THE ILLUSTRATED NINJA HANDBOOK

Hidden Techniques of Ninjutsu

"Ninja is true personification of the Budo spirit"
Dr. Masaaki Hatsumi Soke

Ninjutsu means life,
life means creativity,
creativity is the human destiny.
"Always read between the lines."

Remigiusz Borda

Remigiusz Borda

THE ILLUSTRATED NINJA HANDBOOK

Hidden Techniques of Ninjutsu

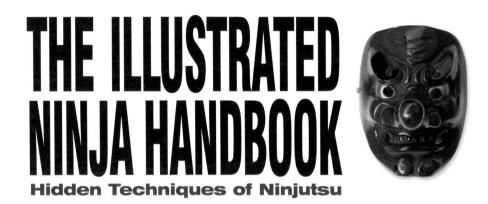

with **Marian Winiecki**

TUTTLE Publishing

Tokyo | Rutland, Vermont | Singapore

TABLE OF CONTENTS

Introduction

The traditions of ancient Japan included the idea of connecting, or more precisely, of not disconnecting the two aspects of a human being: the mind and the body. The samurai's daily task was to work towards self-development. This process of development included all sorts of severe forms of combat training: fencing (with swords, daggers, different kinds of spears, and halberds), archery, horseriding, and various ways of fighting without weapons. A samurai spent the large part of a day on mental and spiritual development, studying classic Chinese literature, poetry, and painting, as well as practicing meditation (Zen). The educated samurai deserved respect — he was effective in battle and admired in the society — yet he also undoubtedly felt good about himself. The knowledge he gained, he was able to transmit to others.

At the same time, other warriors — monks — were developing their skills in monasteries and hermitages on Mount Hiei, near Kyoto. Monks perfected and invented new kinds of weapons, new tactics, and a new approach towards the enemy or the fight itself. They often had the opportunity to test their knowledge in practice.

Over time, people tried to combine these two visions of a warrior. New schools and styles were established that have been passed down from generation to generation in an almost unchanged form.

This centuries-old tradition is taught and developed by Dr. Masaaki Hatsumi. The Bujinkan School is known around the world. The knowledge of the school is rooted in the most ancient scrolls and manuscripts. Remigiusz Borda (b. 1965) maintains and cultivates the art of Ninjutsu. He established a center for promoting, practicing, and developing fine arts, called the House of Arts, in which the Bujinkan Dojo was also opened. He has been practicing both fine arts and martial arts with equal success for decades. He is a highly regarded painter and his work has been shown in galleries around the world. He is also a photographer and poet. Remigiusz Borda is a charismatic and spiritual man. His close connection to nature is not only determined by the fact that he lives in one of the least populated regions of Poland, but also comes from the fact that he is interested in herbalism, chiropractic, and other forms of natural therapy. His metaphysical artistic work helps him in conducting energy psychotherapy and Reiki energy work. Ninjutsu is an integral part of his practice.

In the Ninpo approach, life, human beings, and fighting are treated as a sort of completeness. This approach is expressed in acting in accordance with the rules of the world, nature, elements, seasons, and the principles of psychology. Remigiusz Borda gained his experience for many years through the study of karate, judo, and other martial arts, which perfectly complemented his practice of Bujinkan Ninjutsu. Regular attendance at seminars and training with masters such as Soke Masaaki Hatsumi, Somei Sensei, Nuguchi Sensei, Shiraeshi Sensei, Seno Sensei, and Heinz H. Meyer Sensei contribute to the continuous development his art.

Marian Winiecki

Remigiusz Borda. Still life with fire (oil, 2012)

Remigiusz Borda in his studio. Atelier-Kęszyca, Poland 2011

Remigiusz Borda in the dojo. Kęszyca, Poland 2011

Masaaki Hatsumi. Portrait of Bodhidharma (Daruma)(ink, 1995)

Foreword

The significant growth around the world of the popularity of Bujinkan was characteristic for the last few years of the 20th century. New training centers appeared, one after the other. It is hard for me to remain objective when trying to assess the reasons for this increased interest in this mysterious martial art as well as young people's enthusiasm in seeking Bujinkan dojos. I can only sketch a picture of my love for this difficult art, which now fulfills my life.

More than any other image, a legendary figure wearing black clothes personalizes a young person's dreams of the invincible warrior.

Ninjutsu, saturated with numerous legends and secrets, with roots in the distant history of Japan, still speaks to and creates a legend of warriors possessing superhuman spiritual and physical powers. Those stories, like a magical magnet, attract young people and encourage them to enter the open doors of our schools. As never before in the history of Ninjutsu, thanks to Soke Dr. Masaki Hatsumi, we have access to this great legacy for the first time. Teaching by

qualified Shihan is passed to students all over the world in undistorted form; they are based on the original Dencho. The modern Ninjutsu pioneers, who later became teachers, have acquired this knowledge over the past three decades with persistence by studying under Soke Hatsumi's guidance, or under one of the Shihan, either in Japan or at seminars known as Teikei organized in every corner of the world, during which Hatsumi Sensei personally teaches classes.

The system created by Bujinkan, when combined with perseverance and determination, enables student to achieve masterful skills in Ninjutsu. Taking into account the fact that, in contrast with medieval Japan, we live in a less martial world and we usually live longer, there is plenty of time to practice diligently, and thus achieve higher levels of skill. To do so, one must, as my teacher says, "overcome the lazy dog inside" in order to follow the Path of the Warrior without distraction. It is true that Ninjutsu slowly fills the heart of people who regularly practice this art, transforming their body and spirit. Thanks to qualified teachers, the metaphor of transformation can be explored during almost every workout. This is also mirrored in the name of the style taught in our school: Togakure Ryu, which means School of the Hidden Doors (gates). For those who follow this path and practice the style, the doors (gates) to deeper knowledge open a little bit wider with time. For ordinary mortals, full knowledge will always remain unattainable.

Just as it was centuries ago, today this secret knowledge is still closely guarded from the gaze of the unauthorized. Thus, to open the hidden door one must first overcome the challenges presented by the heavily armed warriors. Images of guards and their legendary power are still very popular. The guards to the hidden doors are as follows: laziness and lack of perseverance, fear, lack of self-confidence, stupidity, lack of charity, lack of respect, and lack of humility. The great truth of a nearly thousand-year-old tradition is still valid.

Today, in the 21st century, if one wants to know the secrets of Ninjutsu, one has to overcome all these human weaknesses. The old shinobi used knowledge of human weaknesses on the battlefield in order to defeat the enemy or to extract from the enemy the necessary strategic information.

Although Ninjutsu is not a sport, it allows the practitioner to attain great physical fitness and to develop effective self-defense skills. But above all else, it contributes the deeper development of a practitioner's self-awareness. In today's wasteful exploration of nature, in times of warfare and social inequality, I can clearly see bright new tasks for the students of Ninjutsu and other martial arts as well. These tasks are as clear as crystal: through the understanding of nature and self-awareness, one might discover latent power in humans, the source of good and justice, achieving the Essence of the Heart, Kokoro no Katachi.

Remigiusz Borda

The Essence of the Heart
Kokoro no Katachi.

You should know that perseverance alone is barely a streak of airy smoke.

You should know that the human path is justice.

Forget the heart full of hatred, greed, feelings of pride,
and the desire to always be the best (with respect to yourself).

You should understand grief and anger as laws of nature,
and try to achieve enlightenment through your indestructible heart.

Never leave the path of loyalty and respect;
follow the path of reason and the sword (Bunbu).

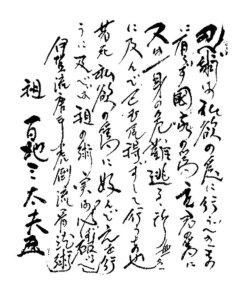

These five dojo rules were written in the new year of Meiji 23 (1890) by Toda Shinyaken Masumitsu.
They were passed from Takamatsu Toshitsugu to Hatsumi Masaaki Byakuryu
on Many Promising Day of March, Showa 23 (1958).
The essence of Shinshin Shigan can be understood through the Kyu and Dan ranks
and through the natural elements Chi-Sui-Ka-Fu-Ku.

Soke Hatsumi and Bujinkan

Dr. Masaaki Hatsumi was a student of Toshitsugu Takamatsu. He not only continues on the path of his great predecessors but, respecting tradition and history, he fits perfectly within the reality of modern times. People are awed by Masaaki Hatsumi's rich personality. He is a highly regarded expert in the field of ancient Japanese medicine, a philosopher, a writer, and an artist practicing traditional ink painting. His knowledge and collective experience are unique and incomparable. Thanks to Soke Hatsumi, Ninjutsu is perceived not as a collection of archaic ways of fighting, but as a real and very effective martial art, used successfully by the special forces of the world's largest armies and by people who want to practice classic Budo.

Soke Hatsumi created within Bujinkan (the name of the school, which can be translated as "Temple of the martial arts God") an excellent training system. The system is based on years of combat experience, tradition, and transfer of knowledge.

Soke Hatsumi introduced new ways of training to the school, enabling students of Ninjutsu to continuously and systematically enhance their skills. Technical and mental development should always be associated with an appropriate teacher. Only a proper relationship between a master and a student is a guarantee that the system, method, and spirit of Budo won't be distorted or lost.

At this point I would like to thank my direct teacher, Heinz H. Meyer, 10 dan Judan Kugyo, for solid training and the heart of a warrior, which he, with great competence and enthusiasm, transferred to me. I direct my sincere gratitude to Jesko Welke, 5th Dan (Godan), for the long-term cooperation in which we both continuously grow.

1. *Toshitsugu Takamatsu Soke (1887-1972)*

2. *Masaaki Hatsumi Soke and Takamatsu Toshitsugu during the Shrikenjutsu training.*

3. *Masaaki Hatsumi Soke with the author (first visit to Japan, 2000).*

4. *Somei Sensei with the author (Japan, 2006).*

5. *Jesko Welke with the author (Kęszyca, Poland, 2012).*

6. *Shihan H. H. Meyer with the author (Kęszyca, Poland, 2012).*

Toshitsugu Takamatsu

Shortly before his death in 1974, Toshitsugu Takamatsu, master of nine traditional Japanese Ryu-ha, identified his favorite student, Masaaki Hatsumi, as his heir. Dr. Masaaki Hatsumi named the new school in honor of his teacher, who, after his death, was called Bujin ("the divine warrior"). The world Bujinkan can be interpreted as "house of the divine warrior." Bu means "warrior," Jin means "god," and the word Kan means "house." Due to the extensive amount of knowledge passed by Takamatsu to Hatsumi — it contained nine martial traditions (Ryu-ha) — Hatsumi Sensei decided not to teach them separately, but to convey the entire body of knowledge as a unity. Of the nine Bujinkan schools, six are the samurai schools and three are the ninja schools. However, Bujinkan Budo is called Ninjutsu.

Togakure Ryu Ninpo 戸隠流

first Soke: around the year 1161

Gyokushin Ryu Ninpo 玉心流忍法

first Soke: around the year 1300

Kumogakure Ryu Ninpo 雲隠流忍法

first Soke: around the year 1550

Gyokko Ryu Kosshijutsu 玉虎流骨指術

first Soke: around the year 1156

Shinden Fudo Ryu Dankentaijutsu 神伝不動流打拳体術

first Soke: around the year 1130

Koto Ryu Koppojutsu 虎倒流骨法術

first Soke: around the year 1532.

Gikan Ryu Koppojutsu 義鑑流骨法術

first Soke: around the year 1558

Kukishinden Ryu Happo Bikenjutsu 九鬼神伝流八法秘剣術

first Soke: around the year 1336

Takagi Yoshin Ryu 高木揚心流柔体術

first Soke: around the year 1625.

Nin (刃) sometimes pronounced shin; consists of two characters

 the person with
a sword (knife) 刃

 a heart 心

The word Bujinkan can be interpreted
as "house of the divine warrior."
Bu 武 - warrior
Jin 神 - god
Kan 館 - home

戸隠流忍法体術 1. Togakure Ryu Ninpo
School of the Hidden Door
First Soke: 1161

In 637 C.E., in the province of Shinano, on top of Mount Hiei, En no Gyoja established Mikkyo. His student, Dengyo Daishi, then created on the same mountain the Buddhist sect Tendai Shugendo and opened the Enryakuji monastery. To this day, the monks of this monastery practice Shugendo and mountain asceticism, which includes practices of purification through trials and hardship. A small settlement called Togakure was located near Mount Hiei. Here, Daisuke Nishina was born into a samurai family in 1161. From his earliest years he studied at the Tendai monastery at the top of Togakure (Mount Hiei). Nishina's experience beginning at that time played an important role in the system of combat, survival, and infiltration he created. It is important to understand the reasons that led to the foundation of Togakure Ryu Ninpo.

Daisuke Nishina's father was Yukihiro Nishina. He was a high-ranking samurai in the service of Duke Minamoto Yoshinaka (a cousin of the first Shogun of Japan). When Minamoto Yoshinaka was a child, one of his rivals sent a samurai who was told to kill little Minamoto and his mother. Mother and child, however, escaped and hid in the village with a loyal peasant family. Later, Minamoto Yoshinaka was brought to Kiso in Shinano Province, near the village of Togakure. Yukihiro Nishina of Togakure served the family of Yoshinaka well; years later, members of the family defeated their rivals and ruled over Japan. However, other leaders perceived Minamoto Yoshinaka as a threat, and many of them turned against him. Minamoto Yoshinaka changed his name to Kiso Yoshinaka, after the name of the village in which he lived (this was a common practice). In 1184, Yoshinaka's half-brother attacked him with an army. Sixty thousand samurai warriors quickly descended on Yoshinaka's army near Kyoto. The battle was called Awaze no Kassan. Kiso Yoshinaka was killed in this battle. Yukihiro of Togakure, who had fought in the battle, also died, but his son Daisuke Nishina survived the battle.

However, because Nishina fought for the army that was defeated, he had to flee. He took refuge in Iga Province, hiding in the inaccessible, misty mountains and forests. He changed his name to Daisuke Togakure, accordingly to the place of his birth. While Daisuke was in Iga, he met Doshi Kain (Kagakure Doshi). Kagakure Doshi was shinobi, and the third Soke of Hakuun Ryu, which was one of the original Ninjutsu systems developed from the teachings of Ikai (or Yi Gai, who brought the foundations of Koshijutsu from China). It is believed that Doshi was Daisuke's uncle and that Daisuke had fled to Iga Province to find him. Daisuke Togakure learned Doshi's way of fighting, and combined it with the beliefs of his own Shugendo system. Thus, the beginnings of Togakure Ryu were forged.

However, Daisuke was not the only one who was taking the precious Kain Doshi's lessons. Shima Kosanta Miniamoto no Kanesada, a high-ranking samurai, accompanied Daisuke. Shima had also fought in the battle of Awaza no Kassen, where he became friends with Daisuke and his father. Shima was wounded during this battle, and Daisuke took him with him as he escaped to Iga. Later, Shima became the second Soke of Togakure Ryu. After Daisuke's death, he took the name Daisuke Togakure II. His son, Goro Togakure, the third Soke, is recognized as being the one who actually fashioned the teachings of Togakure into the Ninjutsu system that is taught today. The 11th, 12th, and 13th Soke of the school were named after the main town of the province, that is, Iga Ueno. It is said that members of the Hattori clan practiced Togakure Ryu. Hattori Hanzo is considered to be the most famous ninja of all times. Members of the Momochi family also trained in this system. The 21st Soke of Togakure Ryu, Momochi Kobei, was a descendent of Momochi Sandayu, the second most famous ninja and a leading figure in Iga Province.

As in many other martial arts schools, control of the system remained with the family who founded it. Knowledge and skills were traditionally passed from father to son. It was not until the 16th century, when the family line was childless, that the most senior member of Togakure Ryu, Nobutsuna Toda, took the leadership position. He became the 24th Soke and controlled the system and training. When Toda assumed the leadership role, he added his own Ninjutsu system, Kumogakure Ryu, to Togakure Ryo. The Toda family also controlled Gyokko Ryu and Koto Ryu; from that time on, all those martial art systems were passed down together.

Shinryuken Masamitsu Toda was the 32nd Soke of Togakure Ryu. In the mid-19th century he was a sword master and sword instructor for the To-kugawa Shogunate. He resigned from his position when he learned that he was teaching swordsmanship to men who were later supposed to kill other Japanese people, behavior inconsistent with the principles of Toga-kure Ryu.

The 33rd Soke of Togakure Ryu was Takamatsu Toshitsugu. He was the last member of the Toda family to control Togakure Ryu. A millennium had passed since the Tendai Shugendo sect was founded.

(Above left) Daisuke Nishina (Togakure), approximately 1162. He was probably the founder of Togakure Ryu.

(Above) 18th century samurai armor. The Takeda family coat of arms is visible on the helmet. The Takeda family frequently utilized the services of ninja clans.

玉
心
流
忍
法
2. Gyokushin Ryu Ninpo
School of the Jeweled Heart

First Soke: around 1300.

Gyokushin Ryu Ninjutsu is a branch of Koshijutsu. It is believed that Sasaki Goeman Tenruyoshi, a student of Gyok-ko Ryu, was the founder of the school. The methods used in Gyokushin Ryu (various blocks, strikes, and stances) resemble those of Gyokko Ryu. Sasaki Gendayu served the Daimyo of Kishu and was paid 200 Koku; later, it was increased to 400 Koku per year. It is possible that Sasaki, like his father, was a highly skilled warrior of Gyokko Ryu. Gyokushin Ryu was secretly taught in Kishu and Takeda provinces. At some point in the 17th century, the school came into contact with Togakure Ryu and the Toda family. When the style was passed to Toda Nobutsuna, it ceased being a closed secret.

Not much is known about the tradition of Gyokushin Ryu Ninpo because the style was more focused on espionage skills compared to other Ninjutsu schools, which focused on hand-to-hand combat.

雲
隠
流
忍
法
3. Kumogakure Ryu Ninpo
Hiding in the Clouds School

First Soke: about 1550.

Combat techniques from Kumogakure Ryu are very similar to those of Togakure Ryu. The Toda family most likely founded Kumogakure Ryu. The ninja of Kumogakure Ryu went into combat wearing just lightly armored sleeves under their traditional clothes. Another interesting fact is that in this Ryu, warriors sometimes wore demon masks. The characteristic weapon for this school was the *kamayari*, a spear with hooks on the side. The hooked spear, apart from being used to attack an opponent, was also used against swordsman in combat in order to parry and trap incoming blades. The Kumogakure Ryu Dencho mentions a ninja named Sarutobi Sasuke who used the hooked spear to leap from tree to tree, hooking it onto branches. Another specialty of Kumogakure Ryu included survival training and the skill of being able to light a fire in whatever circumstances the ninja found himself.

玉
虎
流
骨
指
術

4. Gyokko Ryu Kosshijutsu
School of the Jewel Tiger

First Soke: about 1300.

Gyokko Koshijutsu Ryu is the oldest of the nine Bujinkan traditions. There is no doubt that it is the core style of the majority of the martial arts that comprise the Bujinkan system. Hatsumi Sensei decided that Koshijutsu would provide the basis for the other systems, including Togakure Ryu, Koto Ryu, Gikan Ryu, Shinden Fudo Ryu, Gyokushin Ryu, and Kumogakure Ryu.

Gyokko means the jeweled tiger or the jewel tiger. It can be understood as a metaphor for a tiger's eye. The style's methods of movement and the basic principles of this school were developed in China during the Tang Dynasty (618-907 C.E.). It is believed that either a short man or a petite woman must have created the style due to its characteristic movements. It is known that there was a woman in the court of Chan (now Xian) who indeed had become famous for her martial arts skills. When the Tang Dynasty was overthrown in 907, many Chinese nobles fled and hid in Japan.

In Japan, the names You Gyokko (Yao Yu Hu) and Cho Gyokko were associated with each other. It is possible that they came from one and the same person. General Ikai (or Ibou) is believed to have taken part in the early development of Gyokko Ryu. According to Hatsumi, the person (somebody: bou) responsible for establishing the school in Japan could have come from another country (I).

The first official Soke of the officially established Gyokko Ryu was Tozawa Hakuunsai. His name may also be connected with a style that no longer exists: Hakuun Ryu Ninjutsu. This all occurred during the Hogen era (1156-1159), which means that Gyokko Ryu is the oldest documented martial arts system in Japan.

Koshijutsu means "to defeat an enemy with one finger." Therefore, the school's training strongly focuses on striking with fingers, toes, and leg bones — but with other parts of the body as well. Strikes characteristic for the school include: powerful and dynamic blocks that destroy an opponent's muscle structure; ripping, piercing, and tearing techniques that employ fingers and toes; dynamic stomping kicks, grappling, and throws.

Gyokko Ryu taught students to use as much strength as was needed to knock the enemy down. The members of the school were also known for their sword skills, as well as the use of the *roku-shakubo* and *tanto*.

神伝不動流打拳体術 5. Shinden Fudo Ryu Dakentaijutsu Immovable Heart School

First Soke: about 1130.

Ganpachiro Temeyoshi established Shinden Fudo Ryu in the mid-12th century.

In the school's style, one can notice the influence of Koshijutsu, as introduced by Izumo Kanji Yoshitero. It is possible that Izumo, as a founder of Shinden Fudo Ryu, was the same person who founded Kukishinden Ryu.

The foundation of all the skills in this school is the knowledge of the principles of nature. Nature is used as an ally to strengthen the body: first the legs, then the hips and fists. In this school, no dojo was built; no special equipment was used for practice. Classes were run in a natural environment. Trees were used to practice strikes and breaks. Members, for example, would hit trees with their foreheads in order to make the head stronger. In bamboo forests, members could practice kicks typical for this school only. Peeling a tree's bark is comparable to tearing human skin. Members of the school specialized in Jujutsu and Iainuki. The katana used in Shinden Fudo Ryu was longer and heavier than the traditional one. This made the sword harder and slower to pull out of the scabbard. After practicing this, members of the school had no difficulty in drawing swords rapidly.

It is said that Izumo learned how to use *yari* from Tengu. Even today those techniques remain a secret. Various types of *yari* – *ono*, *otsuchi*, and *naginata* – were taught by the school. The members of the school also practice Hojojutsu.

With a battlefield axe, one can destroy samurai armor; with a large war hammer, one can destroy doors and barricades; with *naginata*, the attack against cavaliers can be conducted.

There are no formal postures (Kamae) in Shinden Fudo Ryu, thus the school is known for its Shizen no Kamae (natural posture).

It was most important for a warrior to land on his feet when being thrown, as members always wore long swords (Daisho). To fall unskillfully with a long sword was always dangerous; one could end up dead. There is a saying that in order to move forward with learning new techniques one must be able to do a half-somersault on one finger. During his first classes under his grandfather Toda, Takamatsu Sensei was thrown endlessly by other students before he was allowed to take his first class with the katana.

虎倒流骨法術 6. Koto Ryu Koppojutsu
Tiger Knocking Down School

First Soke: 1532.

It is believed that Chan Busho, a Chinese warrior, brought Koto Ryu Koppojutsu to Japan from China via Korea. It was probably hundreds of years before the style was fashioned into Koto Ryu. The exact origin of this school is unknown. In 1542, Sakagami Taro Kunishige combined the techniques into one Ryu-ha. He was also Soke in Gyokko Ryu. These styles share many similarities.

Many ninja and samurai trained in the methods of the Koto Ryu. Momochi Sandayu was taught by Ishigawa Goemon, who at the same time was a famous ninja and criminal. Momochi always denied that Ishigawa Goemon was a member of his clan and school. Goemon was perceived as a "Robin Hood sort of ninja," and he was believed to have been captured and boiled to death in oil. Some historians, including Toshitsugu Takamatsu, believe that Ishigawa Goemon was never caught, but the Shogunate was too ashamed to admit it. In many cases, the story, which has passed from mouth to mouth, was closer to the truth than the written word.

In this Ryu, there is one very unique position, Mangetsu no Kamae, in which a warrior kept the sword over his head in such a way that the blade would reflect the sunlight and blind the enemy. Alternately, if it was raining, the blood groove was used to collect the rainwater, which was then flicked into the enemy's eyes.

A further specialty of the Koto Ryu warrior was to look not into the opponent's eyes but between the eyebrows. In this way, the enemy was not able to recognize the real intentions of the warrior. The opponent was bluffed into thinking that he had eye contact with a skillful warrior. Takamatsu Toshitsugu began his training with the Koto Ryu at the age of 9; at the age of 13 he was named the master. In 1960, Takamatsu presented the effectiveness of Koto Ryu in front of a journalist from one of Tokyo's sport newspapers. He did it by drilling five holes in the bark of a tree with just one strike.

義鑑流骨法術

7. Gikan Ryu Koppojutsu
School of Truth, Loyalty, and Justice

First Soke: 1558

Gikan Ryu was established by Uryu Hangan Gikanbo, the Daimyo of Kawachi no Kuni (the castle of Kawachi). It was said that Uryu Gikanbo's punch was so strong he could break a sword blade in half. Tokamatsu Toshitsugu originally awarded this Ryu to Akimito Fumio, who became the 14th Soke of the school. But Akimoto died early from illness and didn't leave a successor. Tokamatsu Toshitsugu Sensei became head of the school, and he later passed it onto Hatsumi Maasaki. The school contains many special kicks, punches, and throws. There is no step-by-step instruction for techniques, and no kata exist in the school's training. Therefore, the teaching can only be passed on in the form of oral instruction. Hatsumi Soke has never publicly taught the techniques of this school because they are are very difficult. The positions used in the techniques are said to be very low, with special placement of the toes that demands great control of the body's balance.

九鬼神伝流八法秘剣術

8. Kukishinden Ryu Happo Bikenjutsu
School of the Nine Spirit Gods

First Soke: 1336.

This school combines many characteristics of other schools that make up the Bujinkan System. Kukishinden Ryu is a branch of Kukishin Ryu. There are presently few lines of Kukishin Ryu, and there are few Sokes controlling them. For example, Hontai Yoshin Ryu has its own Soke. Takamatsu Toshitsugu, Soke of Kukishin Ryu who was given the title as a form of gratitude for restoring the forgotten Dencho, is believed to have handed the tradition over to Iwami Nangaku.

Aikido also has its roots in Kukishin Ryu. Soke Kukishin Ryu taught Morihei Ueshiba jo technique. Takamatsu Sensei also taught Jigora Kano, the founder of Judo.

9. Takagi Yoshin Ryu Jutaijutsu
School of the Heart of the Willow Tree

高
木
揚
心
流
柔
体
術

First Soke: 1625

In 1569, during the Yeiroku era (1568-1579), a mountain monk of the Abe family lived in the Miyagi Funagata Yama area of the Miyagi region. His name was Unryu (Dragon-Cloud). The encyclopedia of martial arts, *Bugei Ryuha Daijiten*, gives his name as Sounryu. He was an expert in shuriken, bojutsu, yari, *naginata*, and taijutsu from the Amatsu Tatara Rinpo Hiden Makimono.

The secret Amatsu Tatara scrolls were kept by the Abe, Nakatomi, Otomo, and Monobe families. Akamatsu Sensei's family also had a copy, as the family was related by blood to the Kuki family. Unryu taught his system to Ito Sukesada, a famous warrior of the time. He was a samurai from Katakura Kojuro in the Fukushima Province. He augmented the teachings Unryu had given to him with those of Hanbo, Kenjutsu, and Kodachi.

Ito Sukesada's techniques later became known as Takagi Yoshin Ryu. He taught these techniques to Takagi Oriuemon Shingenobu, a young samurai from Tohoku-Shiroishi Han in Oku, Japan. Takagi Oriuemon Shingenobu was born on April 2, 1625. He died on October 7, 1711. He reached the level of Menkyo Kaiden when he was just twenty years old. On August 15, 1695, Emperor Higashiyama granted him the degree of Shihan in six martial arts schools of the Imperial Guards. He changed and improved the techniques that he learned from Ito, assembling them together into Takagi Yoshin Ryu. Throughout his life, he studied and perfected martial arts techniques in order to avenge the murder of his father. His father left him a precious piece of wisdom: "A willow is flexible, but the high tree is fragile."

Over the course of history, the style was called different names: Jutaijutsu, Jujutsu, and Dankentaijutsu. The Ryu was strongly influenced by Takenouuchi Ryu Jujutsu and Kukishin Ryu. In the 17th century, a tournament was held between the Soke of the Takagi Yoshin Ryu, Takagi Gebboshin Hideshige, and the Soke of the Kukishin Ryu, Ohkuni Kihei Shigenobu. After the competition, the opponents became friends. The two systems they led were modernized and exchanged traditions.

In August 1908, Mizuta Tadafusa Yoshitaro handed the Ryu over to Takamatsu Toshitsugu. In May 1959, the Ryu was passed to Hatsumi Maasaki.

Kuji-in (the nine syllable mudra)

Over the centuries Ninja warriors developed a system of mudras, that is, a system of symbolic hand gestures based on the ancient knowledge of the energy channels called meridians, through which life-energy flows in the human body. Mudras can be used in almost all life situations. For example, pressing meridians located at the end of fingertips causes increased energy flow in the body. Mudra, a hand gesture, was usually accompanied by verbalizing the equivalent syllables. The combination of gesture and verbal expression intensifies the impact of a mudra.

Through the use of mudras, one can enhance physical and mental capacity, effectively manage energy, speed up the healing of wounds, cease pain, and bring unbreakable peace to situations in which life is in peril. These are just some of the things that can be achieved with the help of the practice of mudra. The knowledge and skills regarding these abilities are considered secret and available for students only through oral transmission from the teacher. This knowledge has remained the subject of oral teaching to this day.

1.**Rin** - *Dokko-in*
(Seal of Thunderbolt)

2. **Pyo** - *Daik-in*
(Seal of Great Thunderbolt)

3. **Tho** - *Sotojishi-in*
(Seal of the Outer Lion)

4. **Sha** - *Ushijishi-in*
(Seal of Inner Lion)

5. **Kai** - *Gebakuken-in*
(Seal of the Outer Bonds)

6.**Jin** - *Naikakuken-in*
(Seal of the Inner Bonds)

7.**Retsu** - *Chiken-in*
(Seal of the Wisdom Fist)

8.**Zai** - *Nichirin-in*
(Seal of the Ring of the Sun)

9.**Zen** - *Ongyo-in*
(Seal of the Hidden Form)

Towards the Target

Sometimes, for the shinobi to get to his destination presented a task as equally dangerous as the mission itself. The order had to be fulfilled regardless of the distance and place. Due to the particular policy enforced by the Shogunate (Bakufu), as well as the system of provinces and roads, it was impossible to travel freely. The large number of guarded gates and control patrols positioned at provincial and city borders demanded a number of additional skills and abilities from ninja. The specific regulations in Japan made it easier for some social groups — such as monks and actors — to move from place to place and to change residences. The authorities respected traditional pilgrimages to holy places and travels to well-known teachers. Authorities also accepted the travels of groups

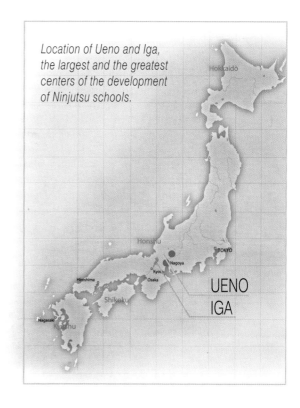

Location of Ueno and Iga, the largest and the greatest centers of the development of Ninjutsu schools.

Below: an ascetic monk, Yamabushi (1), dressed in characteristic outfit. He is depicted wearing a typical tunic and a headscarf that covered the head and face. During wars, warriors often wore armor under their tunics. The monk is armed with a naginata (light halberd) and a sword.
Komuso (2), a mendicant monk associated with Zen Bud-

dhism. Usually depicted with a simple flute — shakuhachi. He wears a straw hat (basket) called a tengai, which represents the desire to move away from his ego. Because the outfit provided anonymity and allowed a person to remain unrecognized, it was often used by ninjas.

of actors who gave performances during the holiday celebrations of different religions. It was quite natural that every ninja in the guise of an actor, musician, or monk possessed adequate skills to make the disguise more believable. Thus, ninjas were musicians and actors; they were familiar with classic literature; they were intellectuals from Buddhist and Shinto temples.

Fudo Myōō, a statue of the deity, traditionally recognized as the guardian of Yamabushi monks. Bodhidsattwa Fudo is stable; his mind is always "unmoved" and not susceptible to temptation of the world.

Yoroi – medieval samurai armor. The copies shown are displayed at the main Bujinkan Dojo. Some combat techniques were designed to be used in cases when an opponent wore armor.

Sensei Sumeia presents a fighting form with the heavy halberd. Bisento and naginata (a lighter version) were the favorite weapons of Yamabushi monks.

Samurai armor from the 18th century. On the breastplate we can see the Tokugawa family coat of arms. The Tokugawa family was one of the most significant and influential clans in the history of Japan. Shoguns from the Tokugawa dynasty often used the support of ninja warriors.

Infiltration

One of the many specialties that ninja warriors mastered was to appear in places where no one expected them. Whether a shinobi's mission was to obtain information or to liquidate a prominent dignitary, the ninja needed to reach his destination unnoticed and to disappear the same way, without leaving a trace. To do so, the Ninjutsu adopted various methods and strategies. Ninjas were prepared to overcome all types of obstacles and security, both natural (water, rocks) and architectural (walls and fences).

Most houses of the time were surrounded by high stone walls. The houses also had towers with windows arranged in such a way that the surrounding area was visible by the guards. Yet ninja, after reconnoitering an area, were able to find a way into the place without being noticed using ropes, steel hooks, anchors, and wood or bamboo ladders to climb a wall. A ninja was able to climb almost any vertical surface by using a metal claw (shuko) that he slipped onto his hands. Sometimes he used similar equipment on his feet. When a ninja got into the residence, he still needed to demonstrate full self-control. He remained invisible in corridors and rooms. He moved silently despite the fact that some floors were constructed so they would creak when walked on. Sometimes a ninja would unroll his own belt (obi), then walk on the belt in order to quietly cross the floor. To walk silently, a ninja might walk on his hands. To move forward, he would first place his hands on the floor then alternate between the left and right foot. Sometimes, a ninja had to suddenly disappear. He was trained to remain for an extended period of time at ceiling level by holding onto ceiling joists or by jamming his feet against the walls.

Some houses belonging to important people were surrounded by a moat filled with water, but this was no obstacle for a shinobi. He was an excellent swimmer. With training he could easily swim with a heavy load. He could stay under water much longer than the average person. To stay underwater for extended periods, ninja would use breathing tubes made from reed or saya (the scabbard of a sword). If necessary, he would build a special pontoon or raft. All techniques were closely related to the season of the year, time of day or night, and weather conditions. The missions were precisely and fastidiously thought through down to the smallest detail.

Osaka Castle (Osaka-jo): construction began in 1583 based on Toyotomi Hideyoshi's orders. The high walls and moat made the complex almost unconquerable for a regular army.

Kunoichi - The Female Ninja

In the history of Japan, there are numerous examples of women who, as empresses, magnates' wives, and female warriors participating in battles, had great impact on their surroundings. Women of aristocratic families usually trained with naginata (light halberd). This continues to be a common practice today. Other weapon training popular with women included the short sword (wakizashi) and the knife (tanto). In ninja clans and families, women also had a special place. They were subject to the same strenuous training as men. Women were effective: oftentimes missions were only successfully accomplished because of them.

In their operations, shinobi warriors utilized the principles of psychology. They used their opponents' smal-

lest defects, addictions, and weaknesses. Frequently, it was easier for women to sneak in and penetrate an area and house. Later, men's weaknesses for women could be used against a male opponent. Female ninja could provide information that was collected indirectly or directly. Just as in modern times, women used to seduce preselected, prominent men in order to draw important information from them. Sometimes the task of a female ninja was to draw the attention of guards so other ninja could sneak in unseen. In other cases, they were employed in the intended victim's house as kitchen help. By having access to food, they could augment meals with rather unhealthy ingredients. Kunoichi often worked alone. It was quite easy for a female to hide an effective weapon. In the Japanese culture, the appearance and styling of hair was the subject of great attention. It was common for women and men to wear ornamental combs and pins in their hair. The pin was a sign of a person's status and origins. Thus, even a naked woman with a whole arsenal in her hair could be an extremely dangerous and effective warrior.

1. Mask of a woman from classical Japanese theater (19th century). Although in the Japanese theatrical tradition female roles were played by men, one could disguise one's identity under heavy makeup or a mask.

2. Lovers. (A classical Shunga woodcut, 19th century). A woman with a traditional hairstyle decorated with combs and pins.

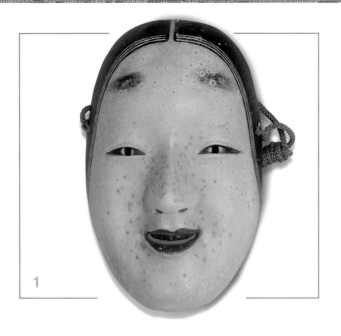

1

2

Japanese hair ornaments were not simply used to fasten hair and keep the hairstyle in place. Women could also use combs, pins, and decorative pins (Kanzashi) as lethal and highly effective weapons.

Women's clothing and haircuts underwent many changes, but the fashionable hairstyles were usually complex and heavily decorated. (Geisha in traditional kimono)

A

B

A. Kogai: small wooden pins. B. Kozuka and kogatana: small utility knives. It was a weapon / tool that anyone could easily hide, especially women. They were usually included in a set with katana and wakizashi.

Tengu

Legends about the origins of Ninjutsu are full of stories about mysterious creatures with feathers and long noses. Tengu appeared in stories about Minamoto Yoshitsune (1159-1189). The Minamoto clan lost a war with the Taira clan and was completely killed off. Only young Yoshitsune miraculously survived the massacre. He took refuge in the wild mountains and forests. The boy, according to tradition, swore to take ritual revenge. He devoted most of his time to training and preparation for the fight. Since he practiced mostly in forests, he managed to damage many trees. As a result, the forest deities became very angry. However, when they came to know the reason for his ferocious preparation, not only did they understand the young warrior, but from that moment on, Sojobo (the most important Tengu) and other deities began to teach the boy to fight with swords. They also transferred secret magical powers to him. As time passed, the Tengu began to be considered the deity associated with the practice of martial arts. Tengu had the ability to levitate, move rapidly, and even become invisible. The creatures were supposed to be aggressive and mischievous. Ninjas told stories about Tengu, comparing himself or herself to the deity. As Tengu, shinobi could suddenly appear in one place, then disappear even faster. Sometimes, someone who saw a ninja was convinced that in reality he had seen a ghost or spirit, rather than a man. The superstitious Japanese, with a culture and everyday life saturated with spirits and ghouls, began to associate the appearance of ninja with something supernatural.

Mask from Noh, a form of Japanese theater. Many theatrical performances include scenes with spirits, ghosts, and other supernatural deities. Shinobis used this kind of mask to increase the psychological effect of fear in an opponent.

Winged Tengu. The mischievous creature presented as animal. Sometimes Tengu were presented as a combination of a bird of prey and a dangerous dog.

Winged Tengu. Two stone statues of Tengu in the robes of Yamabushi monks.

Gotonpo - Training in Nature

Training in nature holds great importance in the practice of Ninjutsu. One Ninjutsu rule says that knowledge of how to retreat and how to protect oneself is a priceless, and superior value. While training in woods, in water, or in open fields, ninja learn how to use the support of the five elements of nature during the fight or the retreat.

Mokuton- Wood
Katon- Fire
Doton- Earth
Kinton - Metal
Suiton- Water

The skills ninjas needed to successfully conduct a mission included: to hide on the ground in grass, behind stones, and other objects to use a territory's feature to one's own advantage, to move smoothly when it was dark, to utilize lights and shadows when it was light, to use fire, blinding powder, and explosives, to anticipate weather conditions, and to use changes in weather conditions for tactical purposes.

Today, some of these skills have only historical meaning, but some elements of Gotonpo haven't lost their effectiveness. These skills are part of the training for special forces and can be used for private protection as well as survival skills. For example: when hiding in the grass we use the element of Doton – earth.

Mokuton (Wood) - Trees

The use of tree trunks to make fingers firmer is an example of typical exercises from Shinden Fudo Ryu. In this school, training didn't take place in enclosed spaces or in dojos, but in nature. Students practiced in forests with rotten tree trunks to strengthen fingers and with flexible branches to practice throws and to strengthen arm and shoulder muscles.

These pictures show the use of the element of wood to hide and surprise the enemy in open spaces, the use of the element of earth (grass, stones, brush, hills, etc.) to hide in fields.

There are many ways to use tree trunks for training. Presented is one of the forms from Shinden Fudo Ryu. When a ninja climbed onto the tree trunk, he wrapped his legs around the trunk and simulated strangulation by squeezing the opponent's ribs, hitting the opponent on the forehead (Kikaku Ken) and striking with the blade of the hand Ura Shuto.

Natural Medicine and Magic

The knowledge of the medicinal and nutritional properties of wild plants and herbs is an important skill in Ninjutsu. Ninjutsu also used to include bone manipulation, working with Ki energy (Chinese Qi energy), and hypnosis. A ninja warrior used to deal with magic using herbs, animals, and object from nature. Today, some Ninjutsu teachers maintain this tradition. When Bujinkan became popular, and Ninjutsu schools appeared all over the world, it became necessary to change this part of knowledge a bit by adjusting to the prevailing natural resources in a given geographical area. This is in accordance with the essence of Ninjutsu, as a principle of Ninjutsu is to adjust to each situation.

Ribwort Plantain
(Plantago lanceolata)
The plant has strong bactericidal properties, as well as the ability to stop bleeding. It is suitable for curing small open wounds.

RIBWORT PLANTAIN (Plantago lanceolata)

Protective magic, endurance, snakes and salamanders, magic energy. It is a very common, edible, and tasty plant. It grows on the edges of fields and along roads. Use in treatments: Fresh plantain leaves stop bleeding and accelerate the healing of minor wounds. Its roots can soothe toothaches. This plant has been used against evil spells. It can be inserted into shoes to enhance endurance during long trips. In locations that venomous snakes inhabit, the root of the plant placed on the ground of a sleeping area will deter uninvited reptiles and keeps them at a distance. The plant inserted under a pillow before going to bed magically protects against migraine headaches.

RED FLY AGARIC (Amanita muscaria)

In Japan, it is called the red mushroom of Tengu. This mushroom is associated with contact with the netherworld.

Use in treatments: It is a common poisonous mushroom. Consuming about 100 grams of this fresh mushroom causes death. However, there is a recipe for a potion from the fungus that provides for effective treatment of painful rheumatoid arthritis. For hundreds of years, red fly agaric was used as an intoxicating substance, often ending in tragedy. Today it is used successfully in homeopathy. There are ancient legends about rituals with this fungus, rituals which supported contact with the netherworld and enabled people to obtain needed information. According to written records, contact with the dead was established in this way only once a year, on October 1, when the wall separating the world of the dead and the world of the living was supposed to be thinner.

COMFREY (Symphytum officinale).

Comfrey was known and used in China and Japan. The plant was known to have power in relationships and financial magic. Comfrey grows fairly commonly in wetlands, in ditches, and on the banks of streams.

Use in treatments: Due to its astringent properties, comfrey serves effectively as external compresses for subcutaneous hematoma and the swelling associated with displaced joints. In the myths, the plant's roots can accrete when cut in the ground. In magic, it is used to build relationships and in spells for attracting money.

STINGING NETTLE (Urtica dioica)

Magic for exorcizing, protecting, and healing. One of the most important herbs; has a long history of medicinal use. The stinging nettle is edible and tasty. Use in treatments: The herb cures anemia, diabetes, purifies blood, removes rheumatic pains, helps in the treatment of prostate and radiation sickness. The plan grows along roads and in forests. Stinging nettle exorcizes negative spells and energies that, thanks to the plant, are returned to the sender. When thrown into fire, the herb repels approaching danger; placed in a bowl of water under the bed of patient, it will scare an illness away.

十文字の構の型

Kamae No Kata - Basic Position

The teaching in Bujinkan starts with the stance (Kamae). Kamae is the beginning and ending of each movement and each technique. Students move smoothly (Nagare) from one position to another. The positions are taught as one continuum of forms Kamae No Kata. Positions in Ninjutsu have a fundamental importance and their use has a much wider application than in other well-known and popular martial arts. Positions are performed without unnecessary muscle tension. They help the Ninjutsu practitioner keep optimal contact with the surface and to thus receive from the element of earth the power needed for combat. The stances also have a huge psychological impact. They can hide intentions or mislead the enemy with regards to the direction the practitioner intends to take. Kamae is therefore a physical spine in Bujinkan. Correctly performed, Kamae impacts the entire movement and, to a large extent, determines the effectiveness of the performed techniques.

Kamae, the stance, is the moment just before the movement. Kamae must be continuously perfected through right positioning of the body. Also, the particular positions represent spiritual attitudes and thoughtfulness of tactics. Great attention should also be paid to these spiritual aspects, because through them Kamae can be saturated with real meaning and life. Otherwise, Kamae will only represent the empty pose, with no connection to the martial art.

Sanshin No Kata - Sho Shin Go-kei Go-gyo No Kata

All Ninjutsu techniques and kata with partner, as well as real confrontations with an opponent, are reflected in the five elements. Each of these elements influences the physical movements differently and has various manifestations in a practitioner's emotions.

Initially, students practice the flow and smoothness of a particular form. Later, students work on understanding and feeling the work of the elements in a technique, using the elements in the movement, and finally embodying them.

On the following pages, the forms of both Kamae No Kata and Sanshin No Kata are presented.

Kamae No Kata

Teaching Bujinkan starts with a stance (Kamae). Kamae is the beginning and the end of every movement and every technique. Students move smoothly (Nagare) from one position to another. The positions are taught as one continuous form, Kamae No Kata.

4. Hucho No Kamae:
Crane stance

3. Doko No Kamae:
Angry Tiger stance

2. Ichimonji No Kamae:
Defensive stance number 1

1. Shizen No Kamae:
Natural posture

5. Kosei No
Kamae:
Offensive
stance

6. Jumonji No Kamae

7. Jumonji No Kumite

8. Ihen No Kamae:
A transition stance, sidestep

8 a. Ihen No Kamae:
A transition stance, sidestep

18. Shizen No Kamae: Natural posture

16. Suwari Gata No Kamae: A sitting stance with crossed legs

15. Fudoza No Kamae: Meditation stance, a motionless sitting stance

17. Hantachi: A half-standing stance (kneeling position)

14. Seiza No Kamae: Natural kneeling stance (the top of each foot touches the ground)

9. Hira No Kamae: Flat stance, an observing and receiving position

10. Hira Ichimonji No Kamae

11. Hoko No Kamae: Bear stance

12. Kongo Gasho No Kamae: Clouds (standing prayer stance)

Sanshin No Kata - Sho Shin Go-kei Go-gyo No Kata

Chi No Kata - The Form of Earth

These are well-grounded stances. The movement is firm, direct, and fierce.

While performing the movement, slide your legs back and forward. Step backward without blocking. Then step forward.

Strike the solar plexus with three or four fingers curled into Shitan Ken.

Sui No Kata - The Form of Water

The movement is soft and smooth.

While performing the movement, slide your legs diagonally backward and forward. Perform a wide movement that comes from the trunk to execute a high block, Jodan Uke.

Then perform an outer hand blade strike, Omote Shuto, on an elliptical trajectory going from high to low.

Ka No Kata - The Form of Fire

Dynamic and more aggressive movement.

Step diagonally back and forward.

Perform a wide movement that comes from the trunk in order to execute a high block, Jodan Uke. Your hand goes back in a straight line to the center. Then, cross hands in Jumonji and perform an inside blade hand strike, Ura Shuto, to the neck.

The Water form and the Fire form look very similar. The difference is in the final strike. When in Sui No Kata, Omote Shute (Picture A) is used; when in Ka No Kata, Ura Shuto (Picture B) is used.

Fu No Kata - The Form of Wind

The movement is soft. A block and counterattack can occur simultaneously.

Step diagonally back and perform the Gedan Uke block by lowering your body and pivoting your hips. Perform a Boshi Ken stab to the solar plexus.

Perform a Boshi Ken stab to the solar plexus.

Ku No Kata - The Void Form

The intention of the movement is to mislead the opponent. Initially, the opponent believes he understands the movement, but the movement then becomes perplexing. Finally, in the last phase, the opponent is surprised.

Step back into Ichimonji No Kamae. Perform the Gedan Uke block. By moving your hand above your head, you effectively grab the opponent's attention. Perform the Sokuyaku Keri kick to the solar plexus.

Perform the Sokuyaku Keri kick to the solar plexus.

Ukemi Gata Taihenjutsu - The Passive Form of Defense

Performing rolls and falls is a basic skill for injury-free training. In the real life, they can save someone's life. Rolls can also be useful in attacks and self-defense: they can be used, for example, when one wants to approach or retreat from an opponent. Through the practice of rolls and falls, students get to know their own body better. The exercises also help students gain self-confidence. Ukemi and Kaiten techniques can be used in almost all real situations outside the dojo. When performing rolls and falls, one should remember to relax the body. The lungs should naturally be filled with air. The body should be rolled up (have a round form) as much as possible during rolls. The interior muscles should be relaxed while the external muscle group should be slightly tensed. Very often, in order to help

So Ku Ho Kai Ten Sideways Roll

Keep fingers together to minimize risk of injury. The eyes are open to be aware of the surroundings.

Zen Po Kaiten Forward Roll

Keep fingers together to minimize risk of injury. The eyes are open to be aware of the surroundings.

Tachi Nagare
(The Flow of Water)

students perform the movement in accordance to such rules, hints such as "calm" or "comfortable" help students achieve the body's desired state. The head shouldn't touch the ground. The body should never be in a position that is too high up or too far forward. Instead, the technique is performed by lowering the body's weight and bending the knees. It is important to remember that rolls and falls should be practiced in all directions and that during the movement students should maintain eye contact with their surroundings.

While rolling backward, the foot that is forward prior to rolling can represent the performed kick or a defense against an opponent's foot.

When the roll is finished, stay flat close to the ground and look around. Then assume the posture. Shifting the body weight from the front leg to the back leg makes standing up into the position easier.

Ho Ken Ju Roppo
(16 Methods of Striking)

The human body can be used in many ways to apply strikes and blocks. Almost every single part of the hands and feet can be used in a variety ways. However, some strikes and blocks are only known in Ninjutsu schools, including techniques with open and closed hands, as well as techniques that use fingers. The use of the thumb is an element characteristic to different Ninjutsu schools.

Some of the techniques are finishing techniques: they might be deadly or they might leave the opponent unconscious. They might paralyze an opponent, and some create an opening for the next attack.

Omote Shuto Ken: Outer Hand Blade Strike

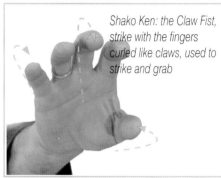

Shako Ken: the Claw Fist, strike with the fingers curled like claws, used to strike and grab

Ura Shuto Ken: inside hand blade strike

Boshi Ken: the thumb strike, used to stab

Fudo Ken: strike with closed fist

The same rules apply to various techniques that use the leg. There are many kicks in Ninjutsu that are quite similar to those of other schools. But the most recognizable and characteristic kicks for the Ninjutsu are the crushing techniques.

Crushing techniques use the hips and body weight. Most kicks are low kicks, with the exception of a jump kick. Commonly attacked points on the opponent's body are: the solar plexus, hips, thighs, knees, ankles, and even the opponent's metatarsal bones.

If the goal is to kick the opponent's head, this is usually preceded by taking the opponent's balance or bringing the opponent to the ground. In Ninjutsu, the adept use of the whole body in combat is why sometimes the knees, elbows, and head are also used (such as at close range).

A strike with the head to the face, nose, or chin.

Kicking, smashing, and stepping on the opponent's foot, toes, or shin.

A one-leg forward kick to hit the head or chest

A two-leg forward kick from the jump to crush the opponent's ribs

A side kick to crush the opponent's knees, shins, or metatarsal bones

A hooked heel kick to hit the thighs, used at close range

Sokuyaku Ken/Keri (Foot Dance)

The crushing kick with bottom of foot or heel; it is used in various situations.

One should practice the forward kick by raising the knee and thrusting the leg forward by pushing one's hips. Do not kick too high. The most effective kick is a kick at the height of the solar plexus.

The kick to the hip while performing Hon Gyaku, a wristlock

Intercepting a kick from the sitting position in order to apply a counterattack to the inside of the leg or knee.

Sokuyaku Ken is a strong kick applied to puncture a target.

During the technique, the bottom of the other foot remains on the ground.

Koho Keri
- Backward Kick

The kick is useful when tori pretends to turn defensively with his back toward the opponent.

During the technique, the bottom of the other foot remains on the ground.

Sokuho Keri
- Side Kick

The body is facing the opponent. The hip pushes the leg forward toward the opponent.

During the technique, the bottom of the other foot remains on the ground.

Other uses for legs in techniques:

Each part of the lower limb (knee, heel, foot, and toe) may have practical use in combat, both in offensive and defensive techniques (blocks, locks, and pins).

Kakato Keri

Heel kick. The elliptic kick with the heel is perfect for combat at mid-range.

Keep your hands in the guard position. This helps you maintain your balance and keep your opponent at the proper distance.

Very painful kick to outer part of the opponent's thigh

A heel kick done while on the ground directed at the solar plexus.

Kakato Geri

A heel kick done while on the ground. A series of two kicks aimed at the face of an opponent who has already been knocked down. Tori kicks the opponent while falling down (backward roll). Both techniques — the kicks and the fall — are performed almost simultaneously, and then the combat is finished.

1

2

DANGEROUS TECHNIQUE BEWARE

Kakato Geri: the finishing technique of a heel kick to the neck. The kick is applied after taking the opponent's balance and applying a lock. Note: this is a very dangerous technique and should be practiced during class only under the supervision of an experienced teacher.

Tobi Sokuyaku Ken/Keri

A jump kick with the bottom of the foot or heel. With techniques performed from a jump, an opponent may not only be surprised by the sudden change of level, but these techniques can also add to the force applied to a crushing technique.

Bend the right leg to protect the body from below. Create the guard with the hands.

The trunk is straight. The eyes face the opponent. Hands in guard will help maintain balance.

The bent leg protects the crotch but also enables the kick to have greater range and dynamics.

Tobi Sokuyaku Ken/Keri - Ryote Form

Typical for the Koto Ryu Koppo Jutsu, a double-leg kick.

The upward kick with the toes or upper portion of the bottom of the feet. First take the opponent's balanced by pushing or striking him, then jump and kick the opponent's ribs

Land on both feet and do a backward roll to maximize the distance from the opponent. When the proper distance is reached, assume the Zanshin posture of full alertness.

Weapons: A Selection for a Variety of Distances.

A majority of people recognize ninja warriors by their particular clothes and the weapons they use. For shinobi, any type of object that might help in combat, create an advantage, or help in winning the fight was a potential weapon. They used a variety of objects and equipment, depending on time, distance (close distance, medium distance, long distance), and individual preferences.

Swords of different length: Daito contra katana. In such situations, Shinobi would usually surprise an opponent with a "hidden argument" during a discussion: with shuriken or metsubushi, for example.

The different lengths of swords

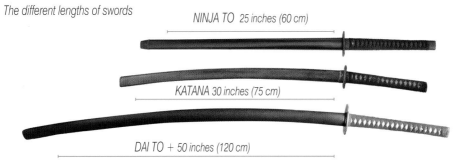

NINJA TO 25 inches (60 cm)

KATANA 30 inches (75 cm)

DAI TO + 50 inches (120 cm)

Other "flexible" weapons (different sizes)

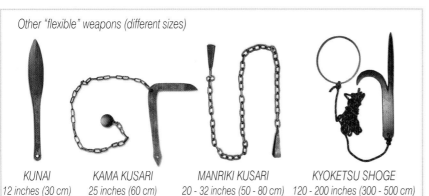

KUNAI	KAMA KUSARI	MANRIKI KUSARI	KYOKETSU SHOGE
12 inches (30 cm)	25 inches (60 cm)	20 - 32 inches (50 - 80 cm)	120 - 200 inches (300 - 500 cm)

HANBO - 32 inches (80 cm)

JO - 50 inches (120 cm)

BO - 70 inches (180 cm)

BISENTO - 80 inches (200 cm)

NAGINATA - 85 inches (220 cm)

YARI - 120 inches (300 cm)

For very long distances, KYOKETSU SHUGO (the different length of ropes) were used.

Bow and arrow was most suitable for targets at long range. It was used not only to hit the target but to set fires as well. Ninja didn't use the traditional Japanese long bow, but instead the shorter ones, similar to Mongolian or Chinese bows.

BO (stick), naginata and yari used at close or medium range.

MANRIKI KUSARI, KAMA KUSARU (chains), etc. They were used at medium and close range.

SWORDS. They were used at medium and close range.

SHUKO, metal claws used in direct contact with the opponent.

SHURIKEN were used for longer distances. They were used to directly hit the target but to also draw the opponent's attention

Blinding powders and other substances thrown directly at the opponent also drew the opponent's attention.

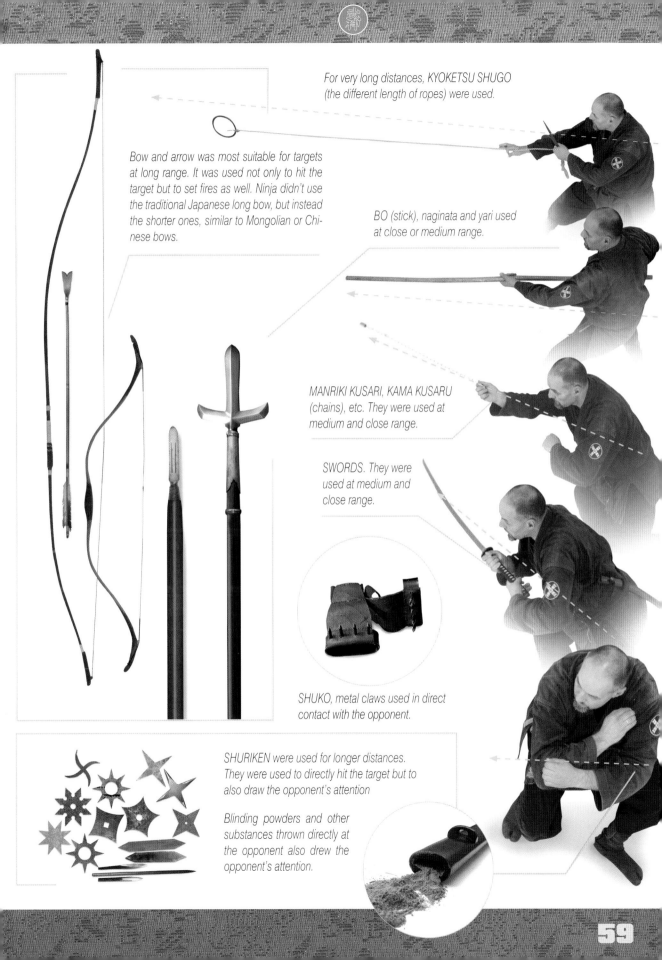

"... to become a good warrior isn't that hard,
it is far more difficult to become a good man..."
Soke Hatsumi

Taijutsu
Body techniques

The fundamental skills taught in Bujinkan are body techniques used in combat. The use of weapons is based on Taijutsu techniques. That is why those experienced and adept in Ninjutsu would have no problem using any type of weapon or using any object as a weapon. The term Tai Ken (body fist) expresses the belief that not only can one use the head, hands, and leg for striking and pushing, but that other parts of the body can be used in combat as well.

In the beginning of Bujinkan training, students learn about Kihon Happo, the eight basic principles. Kihon Happo includes the techniques used against eight basic forms of attack. Kihon Happo is divided into Kosshi Kihon Sanpo-No-Gata (three basic striking techniques) and Hoshu Kihon Goho-No-Gata (five basic grappling techniques). Later, students learn more complex forms with a partner, forms that are particular to Bujinkan Ryu. They also learn kata with a partner from various Ryu included in Bujinkan. At the same time, students are taught techniques and methods for using weapons. In the beginning, they are taught to use hanbo and bo; later, the jo, katana, tanto, as well as naginata, yari, kyoketsu shoge, and others. To master Taijutsu, it takes a lifetime of constant self-development and progress to perfect the use of weapons. Thus, students must show a great deal of humility and persistence.

Some of the principles of Taijutsu:
Shizen Gyo Un Ryu Sui
(Move naturally, harmoniously, yet with energy)
Ken Tai Ichi Jo
(The power of technique results from the movement of the whole body)
Shin Gi Tai Ichi
(The union of spirit (shin), technique (gi), and body (tai)).

Kihon Happo (The Eight Principles): Musha Dori

To perform effective techniques, it is important to skillfully lower and raise the body during the particular parts of a movement. This method is called Ten Chi (Earth and Heaven) and is always used in Taijutsu.

When uke shifts his balance to the front leg, tori steps in and pushes uke's bent arm back. Uke loses his balance.

Tori remains parallel to uke and hooks uke's arm from below. This move causes tension in uke's shoulder joint. Tori steps back with his left leg and performs Ichi-monji No Kamae.

Uke grabs tori's sleeve.
Tori steps diagonally and backward
and pulls uke towards him.

1

8

When uke shifts his body weight
onto his front leg, tori steps
forward while pushing uke's
bent arm forward. Uke loses his
balance.

2

Tori remains parallel to uke and
hooks uke's arm from below.
Tori keeps uke's bent arm in the
position that causes tension in
uke's shoulder joint. Tori steps
back with the leg closest to the
uke and performs Ichimonji No
Kamae.

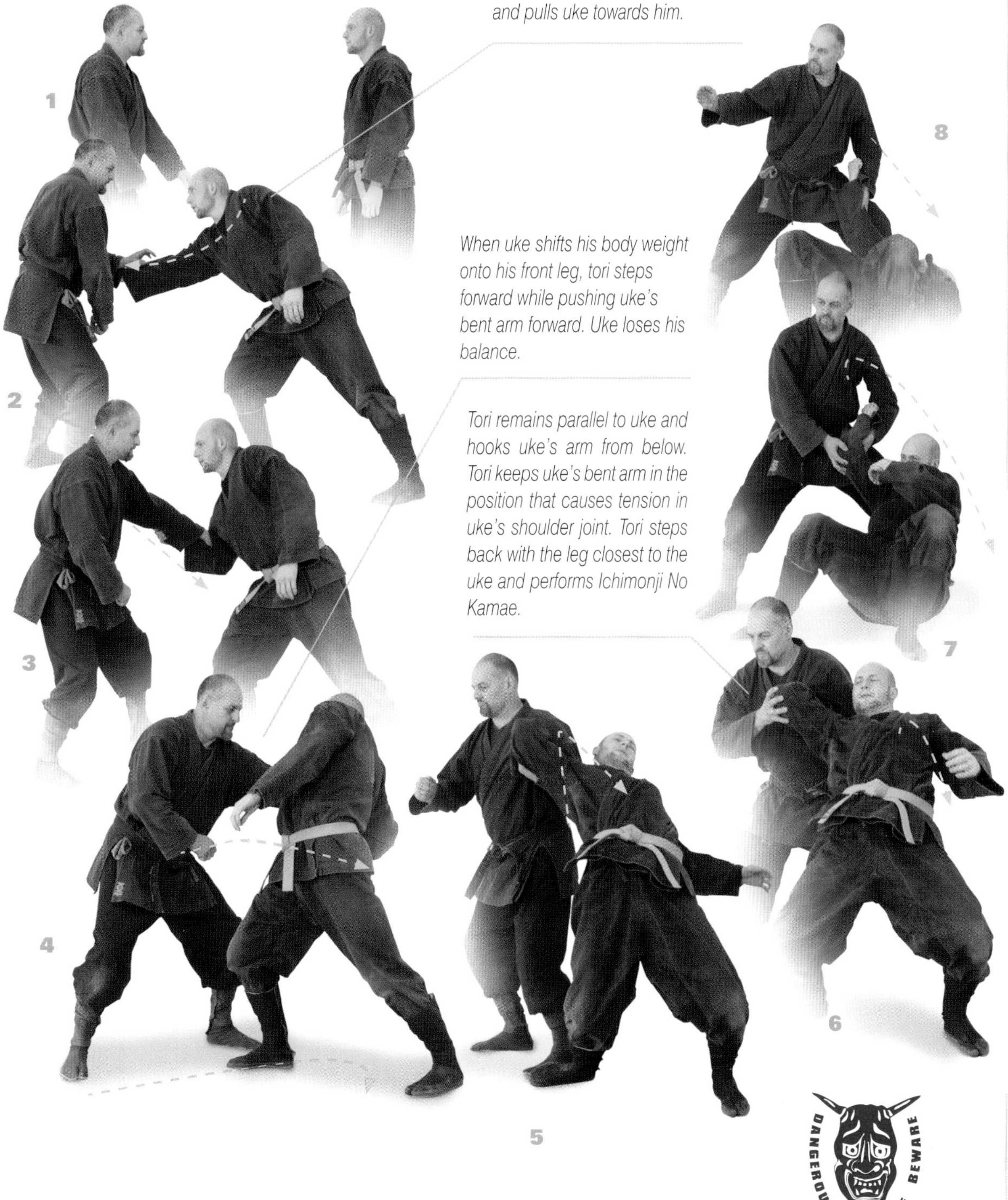

3

7

4

6

5

DANGEROUS TECHNIQUE BEWARE

Kihon Happo Omote Gyaku Dori

A twisting wristlock from the Ten Ryaku No Maki (the Strategy of Heaven)

Uke grabs tori's lapel. Tori immediately controls uke's wrist and simultaneously lowers his body.

Tori pulls uke's hand and leads it high above his head while moving his whole body. While performing the technique, tori pivots his body and shifts his weight up and down (Ten Chi, Heaven and Earth strategy)

Tori twists uke's wrist (Omote Gyaku), lowers his body weight, and moves to Ichimonji no Kamae.

DANGEROUS TECHNIQUE BEWARE

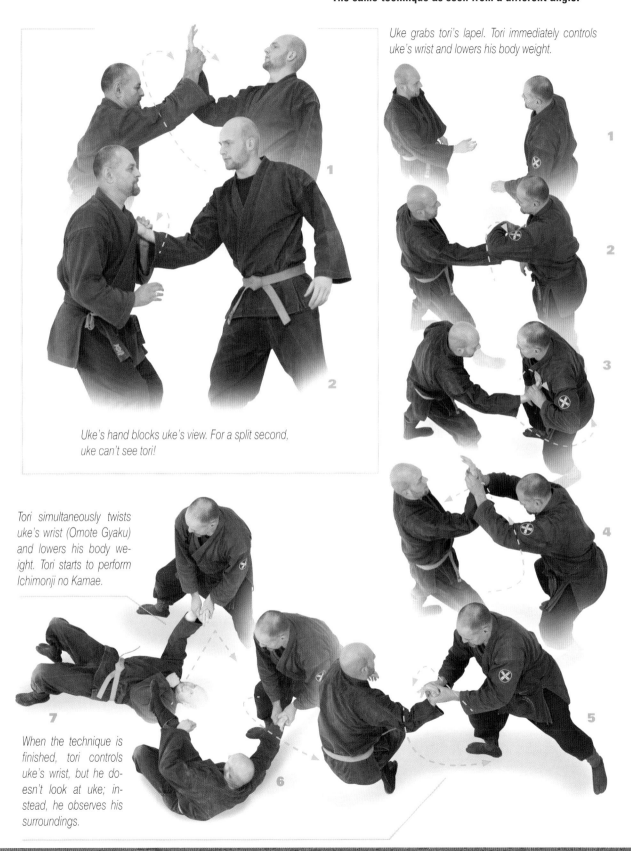

The same technique as seen from a different angle.

Uke grabs tori's lapel. Tori immediately controls uke's wrist and lowers his body weight.

1

2

3

1

2

Uke's hand blocks uke's view. For a split second, uke can't see tori!

4

Tori simultaneously twists uke's wrist (Omote Gyaku) and lowers his body weight. Tori starts to perform Ichimonji no Kamae.

7

6

5

When the technique is finished, tori controls uke's wrist, but he doesn't look at uke; instead, he observes his surroundings.

Reverse Musha Dori

A smooth defensive movement and a shoulder lock. The smooth movement, Nagare, is absolutely necessary in this technique. In order to achieve this movement, it is very useful to practice Sui No Kata (Form of Water).

1

Uke grabs tori's lapel. Tori secures the grip with his hand and smoothly moves backward and to the side.

2

At the same time, tori lowers his body weight and hooks his arm around the uke's bent arm. He applies a shoulder lock with a circular movement.

Tori uses Shako Ken to pull uke down onto his back.

3

4

5

6

7

8

Tori's right hand rests on the uke's chest. Tori moves behind uke and uses Shako Ken to pull him down.

The same technique as seen from a different angle.

Uke grabs tori's lapel. Tori secures the grip with his hand and smoothly moves back and to the side.

Tori simultaneously lowers his body weight and hooks his arm around uke's bent arm. With a circular movement, tori clinches uke's shoulder in a shoulder lock.

With his right hand on uke's body, tori moves behind uke and uses Shako Ken to force uke to the ground.

DANGEROUS TECHNIQUE BEWARE

Omote Gyaku against Omote Gyaku

This form is designed to deepen Kihon Happo (Eight Principles) training. Using the same technique as a counterattack is a great way to enhance the practice of the basics. Tori needs to move smoother and in the lower position.

Tori begins the movement and performs Omote Gyaku as a counter technique (Gaeshi) to the form performed by uke. Tori grabs uke's lapel.

Uke tries to apply the Omote Gyaku wristlock to tori's right hand.

Tori follows the movement but he stiffens his right arm. With his left hand, tori grabs uke's right hand.

Attention: At that moment, tori needs to be very close to uke to prevent uke from regaining his balance. Uke loses control over tori's wrist.

By applying the wristlock, tori gains control over uke. Uke's body is not protected and is open to finishing techniques.

Tori turns and applies the Omote Gyaku wristlock.

3

2

1

Now, tori frees his right hand from uke's grip. Tori places his thumb on top of uke's hand and moves by crossing his feet (Yoko aruki)

Tori turns and applies the Omote Gyaku wristlock.

10

7

8

9

Immobilizing Pin

A series of techniques used in Fudoza No Kamae, a sitting position, and applied to control the opponent while standing up. The technique is typical for Takagi Yoshin Ryu Jataijutsu, the school that focused on combat with an armored opponent. Armor protects from injuries yet limits range of motion. Armored warriors only had a moderate range of motion. The armored warrior used his hips as a source of centrifugal force. It is not possible to bend deeply or perform other techniques that demand dexterity while wearing armor. The initial goal for members of Takagi Yoshin Ryu was to protect the castle in which the Daimio (Prince) lived. Thus, most of the techniques are finished with a pin and control over the opponent, just like techniques used by modern security guards. The goal is not to kill the opponent. Timing is key for this school. In this case, it means that the practitioner initiates his technique at almost the same moment the attacker begins his attack. These skills require vast experience and acute observation of the opponent.

The sitting position Fudoza No Kamae. Uke grabs tori's lapel. Simultaneously, tori grabs the opponent for control and strikes uke's neck with Ura Shuto. At the same time, tori gets to one knee.

Uke loses his balance. Tori grabs uke's wrist with both hands and applies the Hon Gyaku wristlock.

Hon Gyaku and using a straight-arm and pressing the opponent's collarbone.

Tori controls uke with the wristlock and pins the collarbone with his knee.

While maintaining the wristlock, Tori stands and dynamically kicks the opponent in the solar plexus. Tori applies an elbow lock, turns his hips and, by pressing the elbow down, forces the opponent down to the ground, onto his chest.

DANGEROUS TECHNIQUE BEWARE

Intercepting a Kick and Counterattack

Sokuyeku Ken/Keri from sitting position. The technique comes from Shinden Fudo Ryu Dankentaijutsu.

Tori sits in Fudoza No Kamae. Uke walks up to Tori and kicks at Tori's head.

Tori avoids the attack by moving off the line of attack and seizing uke's straight leg.

The counterattack. The kick from the sitting stance targets the opponent's crotch, Suzu.

Tori slides forward and takes the opponent's balance. Tori then moves to the controlling position, Kamae.

Tori strongly hits (steps on) opponen metatarsal bones of the supporting le and blocks him.

The same technique as seen from a different angle.

1
Tori avoids the attack by moving off the line of attack and seizes the opponent's straight leg.

B
Kick from the sitting stance. Kick opponent's crotch, Suzu, or the inner part of the knee joint.

A
Tori avoids the attack by getting off the line of attack, and then seizes the opponent's straight leg.

DANGEROUS TECHNIQUE BEWARE

2

3

4

5

6

7

Tori moves forward and takes the opponent's balance. Tori then shifts to Kamae and controls opponent.

Nagare - The Flow of Movement

Smooth interception of a moving or grabbing hand. The presented example comes from Takagi Yoshin Ryu. This technique may be more complex when the opponent is armed with wakizashi or tanto.

Uke attacks from sitting position. Tori stands in the natural stance, Shizen No Kamae.

Uke's attack comes from the side of his back leg. Tori seizes uke's hand and applies an elbow lock.

Tori completely controls uke. Tori simultaneously applies a pin to the shoulder, elbow, and wrist by pressing his entire body weight against uke.

1

2

3

4

5

6

7

Uke Attacks From a Sitting Stance
Tori stays in the natural position Shizen No Kamae.

1

1

2

2

3

3

Full control over uke. Tori
simultaneously applies a pin
to the shoulder, elbow, and
wrist by pressing his entire
body weight against uke.

4

DANGEROUS TECHNIQUE BEWARE

The Soft Block and Intercepting a Hand

A series of blocks and strikes with locks and grips. The form pictured is based on Ta-inagashi (the flow of body), a technique from Shinden Fudo Ryu. The technique must be performed smoothly and should not be delivered in separates movements. Grips and throws must be performed naturally. Tori, in a natural and relaxed way, escapes the attack. Theory is unnecessary — Do not think.

Uke attacks with a right-hand strike at head (Jodan) level

Tori performs a soft block by intercepting uke's hand (Uke Nagare), and he strikes uke's neck with the hand blade (Ura Shuto).

Tori grabs uke's gi (by the lapel) and wrist, then kicks the inner side of uke's thigh (U Sui) with his heel. Uke is off balance.

Tori applies a twisting wristlock and locks the elbow joint.

While Tori blocks uke's right hand, he also forcefully pushes uke's body to the ground.

Uke attacks with strike of his right hand at head level (Jodan)

The same technique as seen from a different angle.

Tori steps toward the opponent and steps on uke's foot, which causes pain and prevents uke from retreating. After performing the Uke Nagara block, Tori performs Ura Shuto, a hand blade strike to uke's neck.

Tori applies a twisting wristlock and locks the elbow joint.

By pulling the uke's right hand up, tori hyperextends the elbow joint. Tori forcefully jolts uke's body and pulls him down.

DANGEROUS TECHNIQUE BEWARE

Defense Against Opponent's Grab on Back of Collar

The presented form comes from Gyokko Ryu Kosshijutsu. The technique is used in a situation in which uke wants to grab (attack) Tori by the back of the collar with his right hand; uke' right leg is in front. The technique can be used in both static and dynamic situations.

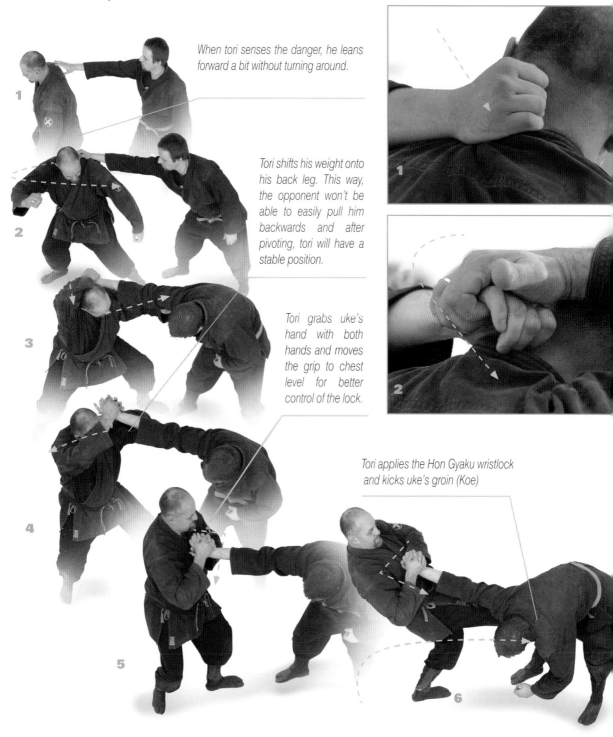

When tori senses the danger, he leans forward a bit without turning around.

Tori shifts his weight onto his back leg. This way, the opponent won't be able to easily pull him backwards and after pivoting, tori will have a stable position.

Tori grabs uke's hand with both hands and moves the grip to chest level for better control of the lock.

Tori applies the Hon Gyaku wristlock and kicks uke's groin (Koe)

The Hon Gyaku wristlock and Koe, a kick to the groin.

DANGEROUS TECHNIQUE BEWARE

Tori uses the lock to pull the opponent down. Uke is face down.

Tori locks the shoulder with his knee. The uke's straight-arm rests against tori's body.

Release From the Grip and Gaining Control While in a Sitting Position

Tori and uke stand in Komi Uchi. Uke tries to hold tori. Tori changes his grip and presses his thumb against the crook of uke's elbow, Hoshizawa. His right thumb presses against uke's neck (Boshi Ken) at the spot when the neck meets the lower jaw, Mu.

1

2

3

Due to the pain, uke loses his balance. Tori changes the grip. Now he controls uke's hand through the wrist and continues to cause pain by pressing on the crook of uke's elbow.

Using his instep, tori kicks the inner side of uke's knee (Kaku) and simultaneously changes his grip on uke's hand

4

Tori changes grip and begins to press the crook of uke's elbow, Hoshizawa.

5

6

Once on the ground, Tori applies the elbow lock with his leg and immobilizes uke's arm between his legs. Tori sits in Fuko No Kamae. Additionally, tori controls uke by applying a lock on uke's pinky finger and thumb.

Tori steps forward and enters the space in front of uke. Tori hits uke's jaw with his elbow. Uke loses his balance.

Tori applies a twisting wristlock, Omote Gyaku. Uke falls down.

DANGEROUS TECHNIQUE BEWARE

Misleading Opening for the Kick

Circular movements are typical for Gyokko Ryu. During combat, tori creates a void, an open space, called Koku that encourages the opponent to attack in a way that is predictable for Tori.

Uke attacks Fudo Ken Jodan (fist strike at head level). Tori accepts the strike and blocks it softly by controlling the opponent's hand. At the same time, tori strikes the bottom of the opponent's biceps, Jakin.

Uke is surprised when tori raises his hands above his head and exposes the lower part of his body to an attack from uke. Uke is provoked to kick tori.

While uke is moving forward, tori immediately moves aside to avoid the attack. Tori quickly kicks (using his metatarsal bones) uke's shin or thigh. Uke loses his balance.

Tori stabs his thumb into uke's body in the kidney area, Shishibatsu.

DANGEROUS TECHNIQUE BEWARE

Moving Behind the Opponent's Back

The presented technique is a form from Shinden Fudo Ryu. The movement should be energetic and fierce.

Uke strikes with his fist from his front (leading) leg, targeting tori's head (Jodan).

Tori moves aside and under uke's arm and then stays behind uke's back. Uke's arm is extended with the elbow facing up.

Tori moves his left leg to the side and back. With his left hand he intercepts the opponent's hand. The distance and timing must be perfect so tori can intercept the strike and the opponent's hand. Immediately, tori strikes uke's face with Shako Ken (the Claw Fist). Uke loses his balance.

Tori moves aside, moving straight forward and under the hyperextended arm of uke. Tori stands behind uke's back. Uke's elbow is pointing up: there is a lock on the elbow joint.

With a quick jolt tori pulls uke down to a sitting position.

4

3

Tori pushes uke's arm down, thus managing to turn the opponent onto his stomach. Tori controls uke by maintaining the hyperextension. Uke's entire body is controlled.

11

10

9

Tori strikes uke's elbow with the Omote Shuto hand blade and pulls uke to the sitting position. Uke's arm remains hyperextended.

8

7

6

DANGEROUS TECHNIQUE BEWARE

The Void Space

Tori creates a void (space) called Koku and leads uke to perform a predictable type of movement. In this form, tori's moves are circular, which is a type of movement particular to Gyokko Ryu.

Uke strikes at the Jodan level. Tori avoids the attack and moves smoothly aside. Tori performs a soft block.

Tori intercepts uke's hand and moves in front of uke, thus exposing himself to the opponent's kicks.

DANGEROUS TECHNIQUE BEWARE

Uke is provoked to continue his attack. He tries to kick Tori's stomach.

Tori intercepts uke's leg, hooks under it, and with a circular movement extends uke's leg. Uke loses his balance.

Tori grabs uke's palm with his two hands and applies the Omote Gyaku wristlock, thus forcing uke to the ground and controlling him the whole time.

Tori moves to the right and applies Omote Shuto to uke's neck.

When uke attacks, Tori firmly strikes uke's arm and moves aside.

Tori changes his grip on uke's hand. Again, he exposes himself to a strike from uke made at the Chudan level.

Soft Block/Reception of Attack and Firm Counterattack

The technique uses the aspect of distance in a manner characteristic of Koto Ryu Koppojutsu. Tori blocks softly just to gain the proper offensive distance.

Uke attacks at the Jodan level. Tori softly accepts the strike and steps off the line of attack.

Tori is an arm's-length distance from uke. Tori shifts his weight off the back leg to the center and pivots his hips to the right to strike diagonally.

Tori counterattacks with Fudo Ken, hitting uke's ribs just below the Butsumetsu, the breast muscle. Tori moves forward quickly and executes Ganeseki Nage, the underhook of uke's arm.

Tori doesn't fight the resistance of uke's arm. Instead, he slides smoothly under the arm and applies an elbow lock.

Tori moves his left leg inside, thus blocking uke's right leg.

Tori doesn't fight uke's arm. He slides smoothly under uke's arm and applies the elbow lock.

Note: Tori doesn't grab uke's hand! His hands stay free, as he may need them when an opponent is not alone or has a hidden weapon.

Tori moves his left leg inside, thus blocking uke's right leg.

Note: Tori doesn't grab uke's hand! His hands stay free, as he may need them when an opponent is not alone or has a hidden weapon.

DANGEROUS TECHNIQUE BEWARE

Tori Exposes Himself to a Kick and Conducts a Counterattack Applying a Wristlock

The use of lock and smooth transition to the next lock. The method of working with the void (space) called Koku is characteristic for Gyokko Ryu.

Uke strikes at the Jodan level. Tori performs a soft block and, in the same smooth move, counterattacks with a hand blade strike (Omote Shuto) to uke's biceps.

Tori opens the space in front of him to provoke uke to kick. When uke kicks, tori changes the trajectory of the kick and uke loses his balance.

Tori allows uke to grab his gi but assumes control over uke's hand on his gi. Now, uke can't let it go.

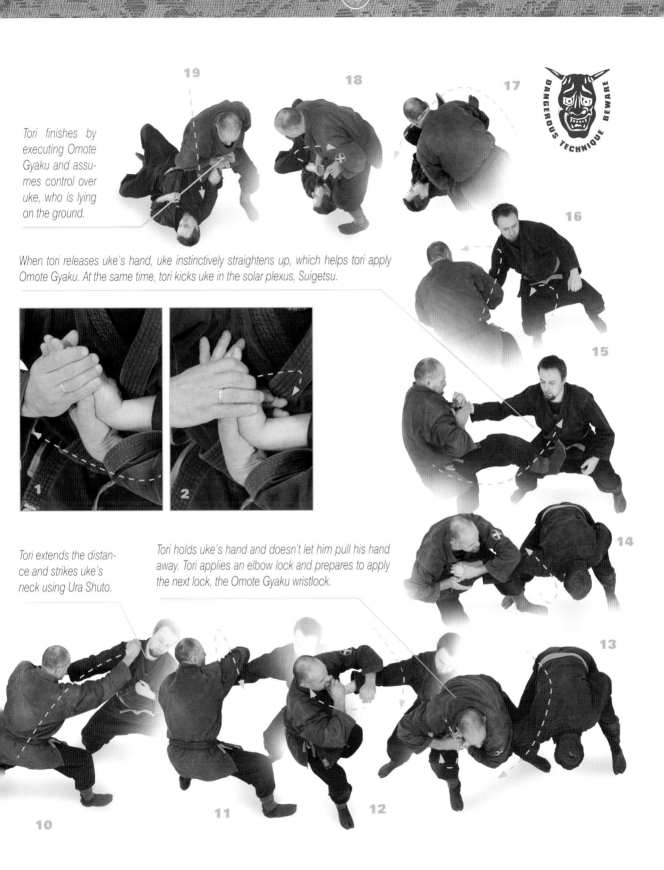

19

Tori finishes by executing Omote Gyaku and assumes control over uke, who is lying on the ground.

18

17

DANGEROUS TECHNIQUE BEWARE

When tori releases uke's hand, uke instinctively straightens up, which helps tori apply Omote Gyaku. At the same time, tori kicks uke in the solar plexus, Suigetsu.

16

15

1

2

14

Tori extends the distance and strikes uke's neck using Ura Shuto.

Tori holds uke's hand and doesn't let him pull his hand away. Tori applies an elbow lock and prepares to apply the next lock, the Omote Gyaku wristlock.

13

10

11

12

Defense Against Grips and Strikes

When a strong opponent grabs one's top (a lapel, a collar, etc.), one must always move smoothly beyond the range of the opponent's free hand (Gyokko Ryu). This is one way to take his balance and open the possibility of causing a painful counterattack (Koshijutsu method). The opponent won't look forward to another fight.

Uke grabs tori's gi. Tori uses a top grip to get control over uke's hand and to keep it close to his body. Uke strikes at tori's head.

At the same time, tori moves diagonally backward and counterattacks with a strong block/strike at Jakkin (this is the weak muscle in the inner upper arm that, when struck, generates a lot of pain).

Tori assumes control over opponent's left hand. Tori brings his hands together on his chest and applies the Muso Dori elbow lock.

Tori brings his hands together on his chest when applying the Muso Dori elbow lock and drops his weight down and to the back. Uke will drop facedown.

ATTENTION: Muso Dori is an especially strong lock. It immediately destroys (crushes) the elbow joint.

DANGEROUS TECHNIQUE BEWARE

Tori applies Muso Dori and drops to his knee, thus moving his weight down and to the back. Uke will drop facedown.

An Attack Targeted at the Legs

While performing the whole technique, a single step can't be missed. To achieve this, tori must always maintain the proper distance from his opponent.

Tori anticipates uke's movement. He kicks with the bottom of his foot.

Tori anticipates uke's attack and blocks uke's shin with the bottom of his foot.

Tori enters the space in front of uke. Then, turning around, he performs a backward heel kick, Koho Keri, at uke's belly

Tori enters the space in front of uke and performs Koho Ker, a backward heel kick to uke's underbelly.

3

When tori finishes the technique, he keeps control over the opponent. Zanshin stance.

12

11

DANGEROUS TECHNIQUE BEWARE

Tori again faces uke and performs the hooking heel kick Kakato Keri to the outer part of uke's thigh, just above the knee. The pain caused by the kick makes uke go to one knee.

10

7

8

9

Tori steps forward and crushes uke's ankle (a lock applied on the ankle that causes uke to fall down).

An Attack From the Air

A dynamic series of jumping attacks is characteristic for Koto Ryu Koppojutsu. Attention: A strike on the neck causes loss of consciousness and can also be deadly! During classes, this matter should receive special attention.

Uke and tori walk towards each other. They pass to the right of each other.

Tori attacks the passing uke by surprise. Tori jumps in front of uke and, while still being in the air, strikes uke with Ura Shuto. Tori then lands on both feet and jumps again, this time attacking uke with Ura Shuto on the other side of uke's neck.

To apply a precise attack from a jump requires that tori have perfect timing and an excellent sense of distance.

The same technique as seen from a different angle.

Tori attacks the passing uke by surprise. Tori jumps in front of uke and, while still in the air, strikes uke with Ura Shuto. Tori lands on both his feet and jumps again, this time attacking uke with Ura Shuto on the other side of uke's neck.

It is important for tori to bend his body a bit and hide his face behind his hand, which is curled for the Shuto Ken strike.

DANGEROUS TECHNIQUE BEWARE

Ambush: The Element of Surprise

This is a technique from Koto Ryu. It has been said that the roots of this style come from China, just as with Gyokko Ryu. In Japan, many ninja and samurai practice this style.

A double-leg kick at the lower ribs from a jump. If the distance is right, tori may fall and crush the opponent's metatarsal bones at the end of the jump.

Tori lands with both feet on the ground and performs a back roll to put distance between him and the opponent.

Uke and tori walk toward each other. Suddenly, Tori jumps in front of uke. Doing this, tori then strikes uke with his hand, which is curled up like a beak. The tips of tori's fingers (San Shin Tanken) strike uke at a point under the collarbone called Ryumon or the Dragon's Gate.

San Shin Tanken: strike with fingertips

A surprised uke steps back. Tori jumps up and kicks uke's lower ribs with the bottom of both feet, Butsunetsu.

DANGEROUS TECHNIQUE BEWARE

Holdfast and "the Demon Horns"

The presented technique of jumping at someone and applying a holdfast is popular in many schools. Below, the movement and the way of executing kata with partner follow the rules of Koto Ryu.

Tori strikes uke's chin or face with his head.

Uke and tori pass each other. Tori moves slightly forward and, being in front of uke, stabs his thumb into uke's neck.

Next, tori grabs uke's top, jumps on uke, and encloses uke's ribs between his thighs. Tori crosses his feet behind uke's back.

While uke is surprised and feels the pain from the holdfast, tori strikes uke's chin or face with his head.

Tori kicks uke's solar plexus with his heel, Kaka-to Keri, and stabs his thumb, Boshi Ken, in the very sensitive place just behind the shinbone.

Feeling pain, uke tries to sit up, allowing tori to release and retreat with a forward roll.

13

14

12

15

11

16

17

10

Tori falls on his back and pulls uke with him. By pushing his legs forward, tori knocks his opponent down. He is on his back.

9

1

2

A Painful Block on the Thigh

Keri Kudaki (kick destroyer) is a technique from Bujinkan Ryu. The technique is based on Chi Ryaku No Maki (the Earth principle).

Tori stays in Shizen No Kamae, the natural stance. Uke attacks with a straight kick to the stomach (Chudan level).

Tori escapes from the line of attack and strikes Fudo Ken to the uke's inner thigh, U Sui. Tori immediately moves to Nage Waza and executes a throw over his lower hip and leg.

While moving to the sitting position Hanza No Kamae, tori still controls uke. Tori hits uke's biceps, Sokki Ken, with his knee. Tori steps on uke's hand to prevent uke from using any weapons.

The same technique as seen from a different angle.

Tori escapes from the line of attack and strikes Fudo Ken to the uke's inner thigh, U Sui. Tori immediately moves to Nage Waza and executes a throw over his lower hip and leg.

Tori executes the throw without grabbing uke by his gi or parts of his body. Tori's hands are free to grab a weapon, just in case.

Nagare - The Flow

A series of movements during which tori neither grabs
nor holds uke at any time.

*Uke tries to get hold of tori's top. Tori intercepts
uke's movement and smoothly guides uke's hand
while moving to the side to the Aruki position.*

1

2

*Uke loses his balance and falls back
on arms that are hyperextended behind
his back.*

3

4

5

*Tori moves to Aruki position (feet crossed): from it,
he executes a fast kick, Asagasumi, to uke's jaws.*

Tori performs a front roll during which he hits uke's Kyusho points, Boshi Ken, that is, a thumb stab in Murasame, under the Adam's apple, and Shuki Ken, that is, a strike with the elbow to uke's solar plexus.

Tori moves behind uke. By hooking under uke's hand, Tori controls uke. Uke loses his balance and falls back on his arms that are crossed and hyperextended behind his back.

Tori executes a fast kick, Asagasumi, to uke's jaws.

DANGEROUS TECHNIQUE BEWARE

The Counter-throw

Typical for this technique is movement on the right side of the opponent, as it was on the right side that warriors wore their katana. The presented throws are executed in the Shinden Fudo Ryu style. They are quite different from what is known from Judo. Before the throw is executed, tori tries to take an opponent's balance by hurting him (tori pinches the opponent's skin, presses his eyes, etc.), then he applies the lock that destroys the opponent's joints. After that, the opponent is thrown over tori's hips and pounded on the ground. The opponent doesn't have the chance to fall on his arms and to protect himself. Additionally, the opponent falls on his own weapon, which under the weight of a body, breaks and mortally injures the owner. Shinden Fudo Ryu uses a combat type of judo. The throwing techniques of modern judo have their roots in such historic combat types of judo.

Tori applies a lock on the opponent's right arm, and with his right knee he presses uke's biceps. Tori completely controls the opponent.

When uke is on tori's back at the highest point of the throw, tori sweeps his hips from under uke and allows uke to fall painfully to the ground.

Uke tries to execute a hip throw. Tori doesn't stiffen his posture but lowers his body and moves smoothly a bit to the right. Tori puts his left hand on uke's hip and his right hand on uke's face (Shako Ken, the Claw).

DANGEROUS TECHNIQUE BEWARE

Now, Tori enters to execute the throw and pulls uke to his hip. When uke is on tori's hip, tori pulls his hip back and lets the opponent fall to the ground.

Half-hip Throw

The technique of pressing and kicking the sensitive points on an opponent's body and performing a half-hip throw. This series of movements enables one to knock an opponent over without the risks associated with having to turn back to the opponent, such as during a full hip throw.

Uke grabs tori in Kumi Uchi. Tori lowers his position, grabs uke's collar with his right hand, and stabs his thumb into uke's neck (Boshi Ken, that is, a small knife). Tori stabs his left thumb into the crook of uke's right elbow, Hoshizawa.

Pressing the sensitive points on uke's body causes uke to lose his balance and move to the left. Tori kicks the inner part of uke's leg just above the knee.

After the kick, tori pulls uke down and controls with a wristlock, elbow lock, and a shoulder pin. A dynamic kick above the knee causes a lot of pain, may even paralyze, and discourages the opponent from fighting.

The same technique as seen from a different angle.

Tori grabs uke's collar with his right hand and stabs his thumb into uke's neck (Boshi Ken, that is, a small knife). Tori stabs his left thumb into the crook of uke's right elbow, Hoshizawa.

Tori dynamically kicks the inner part of uke's leg just above the knee.

The opponent is completely controlled. He is face down on the ground and is immobilized. His right hand and arm is locked in a wristlock and elbow lock.

After the kick, tori pulls uke down and controls with a wristlock, elbow lock, and shoulder pin.

DANGEROUS TECHNIQUE BEWARE

Omote Onikudaki

Gyaku Gi, the soft twisting techniques. The presented technique is very often used when disarming an opponent. Weapons could include the tanto, jutte, or other short wooden weapon (in modern circumstances, it could be a baseball bat).

Uke attacks with a straight fist strike at head level from the same side as his front leg, Fudo Ken Jodan.

Tori steps over uke's leg, lowers his position, and rotates his hips. Feeling the lock, uke moves to the ground. Tori controls uke's shoulder. Tori shifts his weight onto his knee and the hip that is perpendicular to the ground.

Uke attacks Fudo Ke Jodan (a straight fist strike at head level from the side of uke's leading leg).

The same technique as seen from a different angle.

After blocking uke's strike, tori applies a shoulder lock.

Tori moves over uke's leg, lowers his position, and rotates his hips. Feeling the lock, uke drops to the ground.

Tori controls uke's shoulder with his knee and controls uke's elbow with his thumb.

DANGEROUS TECHNIQUE BEWARE

The Misleading Escape From the Attack and the Ganseki Otoshi Throw With One Hand

The presented sequence shows movement characteristic of Shinden Fudo Ryu Dankentaijutsu. Tori stays in the natural stance, Shinzen No Kamae, which is a typical receiving stance for the Shinden Fudo Ryu Dunkentaijutsu.

Tori disappears from uke's line of sight. When tori stands up, he strikes uke's jaw from below, Kudo Ken.

Uke strikes Fudo Ken at the Jodan level. Tori immediately drops his body and avoids uke's strike. When Tori dynamically stands up, he strikes Kudo Ken to uke's jaw (Asagasumi).

These forms require tori to use more initial force and to perfect his command of the Earth element.

1

2

3

Tori moves his hips under uke and kicks uke's left leg with his right leg. After finishing the technique, tori stands in Zanshin, an observing stance.

11

Tori grabs uke's top and executes Gankseki Otoshi.

10

7

8

9

DANGEROUS TECHNIQUE BEWARE

Yoroi: The Techniques in Armor.

The Bujinkan tradition includes schools in which techniques were created and then used for hundreds of years. Samurai, servants, and ordinary soldiers often wore additional protective clothes. People from different places in society and different hierarchal levels wore different types of armor. Beginning with very light protection for the front of the body (kirys do), to armor made of metal rings (ring armor), to the more complicated structures that almost covered the entire body, including the face. With its characteristic structure of flexible design, Yoroi enabled the person wearing it to move quite freely, despite the armor. Techniques used in combat involving full armor were mostly developed by the Kukishinden and Takagi Yoshine Ryu. Thus, when practicing the techniques from these traditions today, one should move as if wearing armor.

In each Bujinkan school, various types of protection was used — partial protectors or ring armor — all depending on the practitioners' needs. Shinobi warriors quite often wore light ring armor under their regular clothes, Ninja warriors also protected their arms and wrists, wearing metal sleeves.

- *Steel shins protectors (Suneate) (A) and Throat and neck protectors (Hambo) (B/C)*
- *A flexible sleeve (Kote) comprised of ring armors, steel shells and the forged part for the forearm (D).*

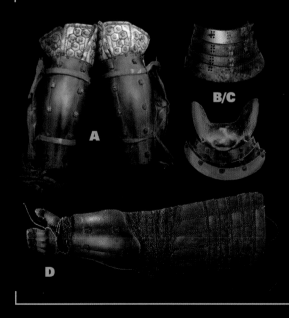

A

B/C

D

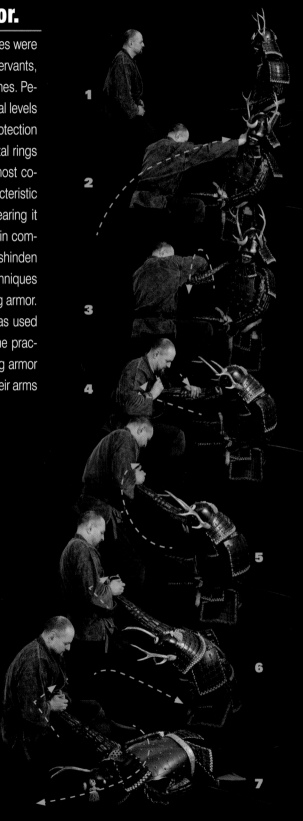

1

2

3

4

5

6

7

Punches and kicks were useless; they often caused pain to the person who struck. That is why the practice of Taijutsu in armor focuses on taking the balance, knocking the opponent to the ground, and then immobilizing him or pushing a weapon blade into the gap between the protective plates. Commonly used techniques included half-hip throws, locks, and gripping armor with fingers. When striking with the hand blade, the strike is usually targeted at the temple (Kasumi) or is targeted to take the opponent's balance. Strikes directed at arms are mostly executed to block and to prevent the opponent's hand from reaching for his weapon.

The Kukishinden Ryu Bikenjutsu provided a highly effective method for learning how to use the ninjato. In the old days, many schools influenced each other and learned from the experiences of each other. And so the Kukishinden Ryu Bikenjutsu influenced the Katori Shinto Ryu, Kanemaki Ryu, and Itto Ryu. The Kukishinden Ryu Bikenjutsu were mainly influenced by schools such as the Iga Ryu and the Yagyu Ryu.

Throw over the Knee

This series of techniques come from Shinden Fudo Ryu. One of the principles of the school says: "When the opponent uses violence against you, remain steady, cause pain, respond firmly and forcefully…"

Uke grabs tori's top. Tori lowers his body and grabs uke on the side.

Tori pulls uke towards him and strikes with his head, Kikaku Ken, to uke's face or jaw. Twisting uke's skin, tori leads uke to the left side. When uke loses his balance, tori kneels on his left knee and throws uke over his right leg.

When finishing, Tori pushes his knee into uke's biceps and arm bone. In the case of this type of throw, the opponent usually falls painfully to the ground and is not willing to fight any more.

Uke grabs tori's top. Tori lowers his body and grabs uke's side.

Tori pulls uke towards him and strikes with his head, Kikaku Ken, to uke's face or jaw.

Twisting uke's skin, tori leads uke to the left side and uke loses his balance.

When finishing, Tori pushes his knee into uke's biceps and arm bone.

DANGEROUS TECHNIQUE BEWARE

Open Stance (Koku) and Soft Undercut

Tori's opening position will encourage the opponent to attack in a way tori can easily predict and can use to take the opponent's balance.

Tori remains in a position that creates Koku, a void (space) in front of him, thus making tori an easy target to attack. Uke kicks Sokuyaku Ken (a crushing kick with the bottom of the foot).

Tori moves to the right and closes the distance to uke. Tori performs a soft block (Happa Ken) with both his hands and then pushes uke's leg down.

The undercut should be performed just above the ground and along the opponent's foot axis.

Tori softly undercuts uke's leg by turning to the right.

The same technique as seen from a different angle.

1

Tori stands in open stance, Koku giving the impression of being an easy target.

2

Tori performs a soft block Happa Ken with both his hands and then pushes uke's leg down.

3

4

5

6

7

7

8

9

Tori finishes in Zanshin stance (observation and focus).

DANGEROUS TECHNIQUE BEWARE

Happo Keri and Keri Kudaki

A series of kicks: "destroyer of legs and arms." This series of kicks used in Ninjutsu has its origins in China.

Tori's natural stance, Shizentai, provokes uke to attack with a fist strike to the face

Tori performs a front kick with the base of the toes. The kick targets the armpit, triceps, or hip joint (causing damage).

When coming down, tori's leg naturally tramples the opponent's knee and then slides down to the metatarsal bones.

By stepping on uke's foot, tori prevents uke from moving away and maintains the distance between tori and uke necessary to finish the technique.

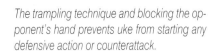

The trampling technique and blocking the opponent's hand prevents uke from starting any defensive action or counterattack.

It is important that the initial straight rear-leg kick with the base of the toes is not performed with tori's hips moving backwards.

In addition, tori's left hand blocks and pushes aside the opponent's arm. It opens uke and leaves space for further attacks.

A strong kick with the back leg to the opponent's hip finishes the series of kicks. Tori performs the kick with the rear leg to the arm, knee, metatarsal bones, and, finally, to the hip joint, thus breaking the pelvic bones.

The Sacrifice Throw: Counterattack to Choking

There are many variations of this form. The Takagi Yoshine Ryu Jutaijutsu, a school of security guards in the Shogunate castle, brought these amazing kicks to perfection. Formerly, this school's students trained with yoroi (armor). All levels of Takagi Yoshine Ryu Jutaijutsu train on Bujinkan mats.

Uke tries to choke tori, a move called Hon Jime Tori. Tori lowers his body and blocks the choking. Tori grabs uke under uke's elbows. Tori strongly presses uke's elbows with his thumbs and fingers. This helps tori to lift uke's arms.

Tori places his right foot at uke's groin and, at the same time, tori drops his body straight to the ground. Tori throws uke over his head, a sort of Tomo-nage.

Tori continue to controls uke's arms, which prevents uke from doing a soft front roll. Uke is pulled down with strong force.

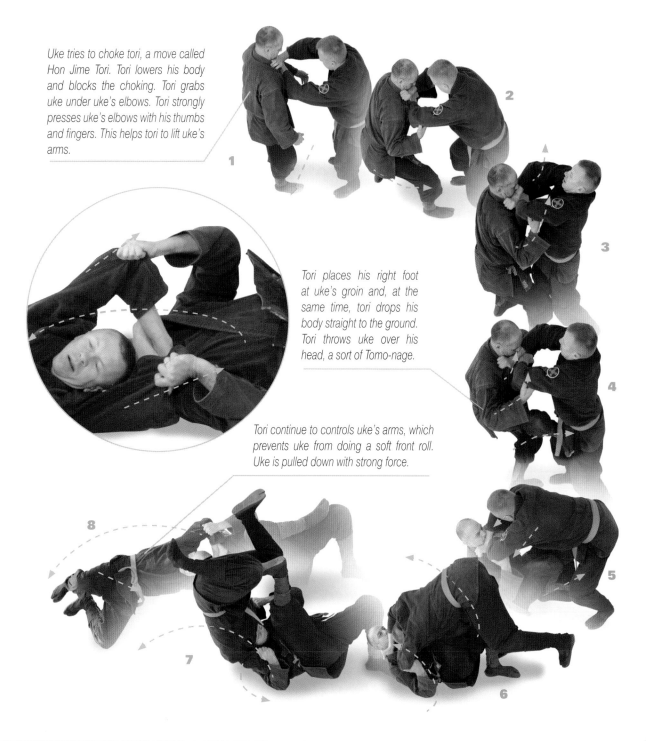

Tori lowers his body and uses his chin to block the choke. Tori grabs uke's elbows and by stabbing his thumbs and fingers in the elbow joint, lifts uke's arms.

Tori places his right foot at uke's groin and, at the same time, tori drops his body straight to the ground. Tori throws uke over his head, a sort of Tomo-nage.

Tori controls uke's arms, which prevent uke from doing a front roll. Uke is pulled down with strong force.

DANGEROUS TECHNIQUE BEWARE

Fourfold Oxygen Deprivation

This is a series of many difficult techniques: strikes, chokes, balance breaking, Kamae structure breaking, entering the opponent's space, and smashing the opponent with body weight.

Uke grabs tori's top with two hands. Tori lowers his body and applies with both hands a fast fist strike in Ikkin (the sensitive spot just above the elbow and below the biceps).

Tori strikes with two fists, called Shiken Ken (a Secret Spear), to the opponent's Adam's apple, Tokotsu, and then applies a choking technique, Hon Jime.

Tori's buttocks hit uke's chest. Uke can't breathe.

Tori seizes uke's hips; uke is off balance and leaning backwards. This might injure uke's lower back.

The same technique as seen from a different angle.

Tori moves forward seizing uke's hips and taking uke's balance. Uke is knocked down. Tori maintains the chokehold.

Tori applies Shiken Ken (a fist strike called Secret Spear) to the opponent's Adam's apple, Tokotsu. Tori applies the Hon Jime choking technique.

When seizing uke's hips, tori puts his entire body weight on uke. This can cause lower back injury.

This technique must only be practiced under the supervision of an experienced teacher.

DANGEROUS TECHNIQUE BEWARE

Tori hits his buttocks against uke's chest. Uke loses his breath. In this movement, tori very often breaks uke's ribs. When uke falls down, he hits his head against the ground. This can often cause concussion or even death.

A Lopsided Duet

Tori must stay calm, as he needs perfect timing and a steady mind. The technique requires the perfect ability to move while in a sitting position. It's not an easy task for taller and heavier people; it's easier for smaller people and those accustomed to sitting in Seiza.

Uke has a wakizashi. He approaches tori and kicks at tori's head with Sokiyaku Keri. Tori sits in Fudoza No Kamae. He moves to the right and blocks Jodan Uke.

Tori pushes uke's elbow and leads it to the ground. He blocks uke's arm with a knee and disarms uke, thus controlling the blade of the wakizashi.

Uke cuts from above, targeting the head. Tori moves to the left and intercepts uke's hand.

The same technique as seen from a different angle.

Uke has a wakizashi. He approaches tori and kicks at tori's head with Sokiyaku Keri.

Uke cuts from above, targeting the head. Tori moves to the left and intercepts uke's hand. Tori gets to his knee (Hanza No Kamae) and with his foot blocks uke's right foot and applies the Muso Dori elbow lock.

The elbow lock is performed by Tori with his leg. Tori controls the blade of the wakizashi.

1

2

3

4

5

6

7

8

DANGEROUS TECHNIQUE BEWARE

Koppojutsu: The Defense Against Wakizashi

Techniques and methods of movement used in the school of the Koto Ryu Koppo Jutsu. Characteristic is the use of various distances from the opponent as well as diagonal strikes. Long distance is used mostly in cases when the opponent is armed.

Armed with wakizashi, uke performs Tsuki at the Chudan level. Tori moves to the right and strikes Shako Ken diagonally to uke's right arm. Tori seizes the arm and moves immediately towards it.

Tori changes hands, grabs the tsuka, pulls uke's wrist, and exposes the inner side of the wrist to hit it with a fist. Uke loses his weapon.

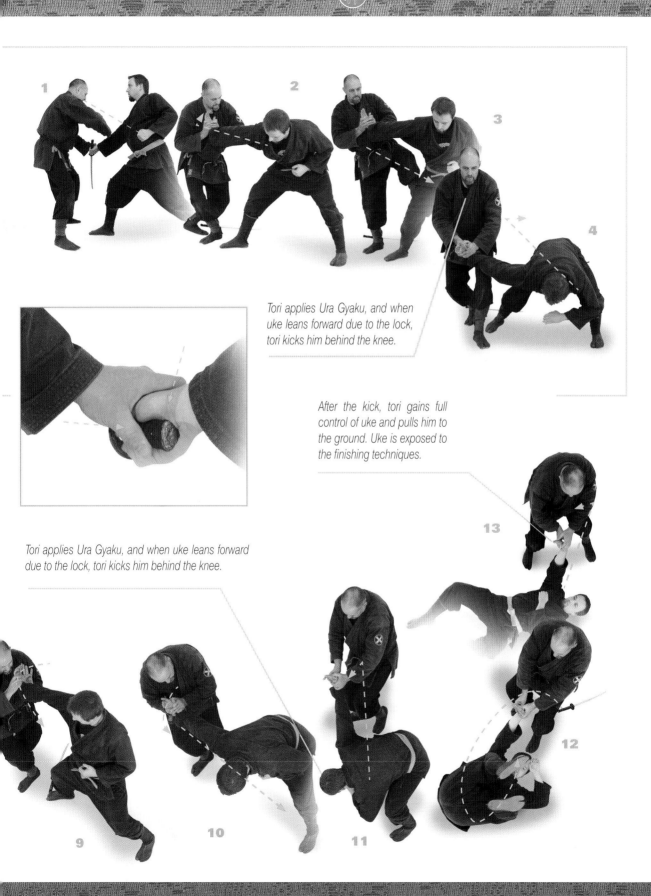

Tori applies Ura Gyaku, and when uke leans forward due to the lock, tori kicks him behind the knee.

After the kick, tori gains full control of uke and pulls him to the ground. Uke is exposed to the finishing techniques.

Tori applies Ura Gyaku, and when uke leans forward due to the lock, tori kicks him behind the knee.

Shin Chu: The Center of the Heart

Engaging in combat with an armored opponent is always the solution of last resort. Without a weapon, one should always takes into consideration the possibility of getting a weapon or something that may function as a weapon. Or simply consider the possibility of escape.

While walking, the uke, armed with a wakizashi, applies Tsuki.

Tori moves slightly to the left and quickly kicks uke's forearm with his shin.

Jumping at the opponent should be executed when uke is falling down.

Uke drops the weapon. Tori immediately enters the space in front of uke and strikes Happa Ken to the middle of the breastbone (which is, in Shin Chu, the center of the heart).

Tori moves to the left and dynamically kicks the opponent's forearm with his shin.

The kick to the opponent's arm requires great timing. The distance between tori and the opponent should be safe. At the same time, the distance should be close enough to perform the kick such that tori can enter the space in front of the opponent. The kick and step forward should happen in one smooth movement.

When uke falls down, tori jumps at him and onto his chest and performs a technique of choice, perhaps choking.

Jumping at the opponent should be executed when uke is falling down. A delay in executing this part of the technique could cause danger, as the opponent could still be conscious and might have a hidden weapon that he could use.

Metsubushi

The use of blinding powder. In its simplest form, the powder was a mixture of wood chips with some sort of hot spice, perhaps pepper. Powder was carried by warriors in their inner top pocket. The powder was enclosed in eggshells. Prior to employing it, the warrior took the eggshell containing the malicious content in his hand, crushed it, and then threw it at the eyes of his opponent(s). Ninja, taking advantage of the momentary surprise, quickly retreated. Using the principle of Earth element, he would hide in high grass, reeds, or blend in with the environment. The blinding powder could also be hidden in a specially crafted sword scabbard, which was used to blow (project) the powder. Sometimes, the ninja warrior would throw the powder at the opponent with a great sweeping movement of the saya (scabbard), which was filled with the powder.

Tori uses the blinding powder Metsubushi at the end of the combat. The opponent is blinded after the throw.

The use of blinding powder Metsubushi. Tori uses the blinding powder to disarm the opponent.

DANGEROUS TECHNIQUE BEWARE

The basic ways of storing and using Metsubushi blinding powder: the sword's tsuba and eggshells.

Metsubushi 1 - Morning Mist

The presented form (kata) shows the way a ninja prepares for an escape or retreat to shelter (which could be taller grass or the corner of a building). The form doesn't look difficult, but in reality it belong to the "royal class" of techniques in Taijutsu. Timing, skillfulness, softness, and firmness, all at the same time. Avoiding open conflict. Escape. These are all tactics typical for the school of the Togakure Ryu Ninpo.

Uke is armed with a katana. He cuts from above to tori's head, Jodan Kiri.

Tori moves slightly to the left and strikes uke's right hand at Ura Gyaku, a point on uke's wrist.

Uke loses his grip on the weapon and receives a strike to the lower ribs (Butsumetsu, the Day of Buddha Death). Tori immediately jumps away, out of the weapon's range.

DANGEROUS TECHNIQUE BEWARE

When the opponent regains the possibility to attack, tori throws the blinding powder Metsubushi in to his eyes.

The same technique as seen from a different angle.

Uke armed with a katana performs Jodan Giri, a cut from above to the head.

Tori moves slightly to the left and strikes uke's right hand at Ura Gyaku, a point on uke's wrist.

Tori keeps an eggshell containing the blinding powder in his right hand. Tori crushes the eggshell when he strikes uke's wrist.

Uke's one hand lets go of the weapon. Uke receives a strike to Butsumetsu (the Day of Buddha Death), the lower ribs. Tori jumps out of range of the weapon.

When the opponent regains the possibility to attack, tori throws the blinding powder Metsubushi in his eyes.

While the opponent can't see anything, Ninja quickly escapes or hides in nearby tall grass. He seems to disappear off the face of the earth.

Ninja would put blinding powder into the fragile eggshells of small birds, such as the partridge.

Metsubushi 2 - Incapacitation

The presented technique is an example of using blinding powder in combat. This form comes from the school of Togakure Ryu.

Uke performs Jodan Giri, a straight cut to the head.

Tori moves off the line of attack to the left and to the side. Tori hits uke's right forearm with his left fist.

At the same time, tori intercepts uke's right arm, applies the Muso Dori elbow lock, and throws the blinding powder Metsubushi at uke's face. Uke, being surprised, loses control over the situation.

Attention: performing this technique requires great timing and smooth movements that come with many years of training.

12

13

11

10

Maintaining the lock, tori leads uke to the ground and forces him to lie on the katana.

9

Tori controls uke with the pin. Uke lies on the katana. Tori gains control of uke's hand and uke's katana.

6

8

7

Tori controls uke's hand. He kicks uke's weapon hand at the wrist. When uke loses the weapon, tori strikes Fudo Ken to uke's jaw, which helps tori apply the lock on the arm.

Doko No Kamae: The Angry Tiger

A series of techniques that teaches a Bujinkan principle: leading and pushing the opponent in a chosen direction (towards some object, for example) through the use of a lock in order to put uke in an even worse position.

Uke performs Shomen Kiri, a straight cut from above his head.

Tori moves to the side and slightly to the left and strikes the opponent's right forearm with his fists (first with left then with right). The opponent loses his grip on the weapon.

While controlling uke's body, tori grips uke's left hand and moves under it to uke's left side.

DANGEROUS TECHNIQUE BEWARE

Tori moves to the side and slightly to the left and strikes the opponent's right forearm with his fists (first with left then with right).

Tori uses his elbow to take uke's balance, or strike uke's head, neck, or ribs.

This move creates a painful wristlock. Tori throws uke to the ground onto the weapon.

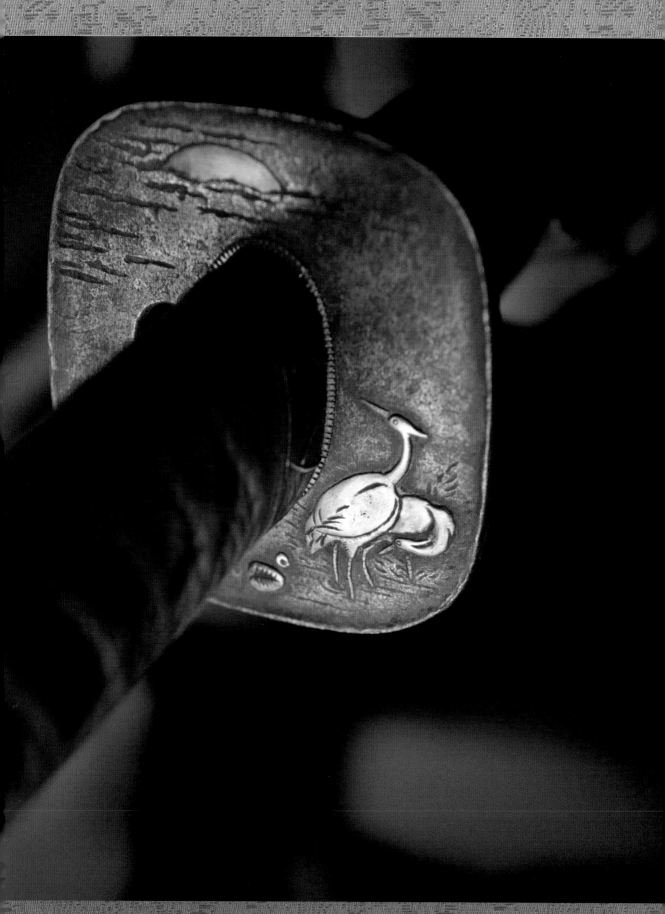

Sword

Ninjato

Shinobito

Shinobiken

The History of Ninjato

The ninjato has the same roots as the samurai sword. There are many misconceptions with regard to the appearance of the ninjato. The truth is that any sword that belongs to a ninja automatically becomes ninjato. Ninja warriors often had difficulty in obtaining high quality blades. They commonly gathered abandoned swords found on the battlefield. These were then converted and shortened. At that time, this procedure was forbidden and severely punished.

Ninja warriors were very creative: a sword in their hands became a multi-functional tool. As they didn't follow the Code of Bushido (Way of the Warrior), they used swords in many unconventional ways. There were known to be swords with one side of the blade having the form of a saw, but the most common swords had a blade that was straight or had a slight curve. The swords of the ninja warriors were shorter than regular swords. This gave the warriors an advantage when pulling a sword from a scabbard. The empty space in the saya (the scabbard) was used to store blinding powder or other useful objects for combat.

Totoku Hyoshi No Kamae

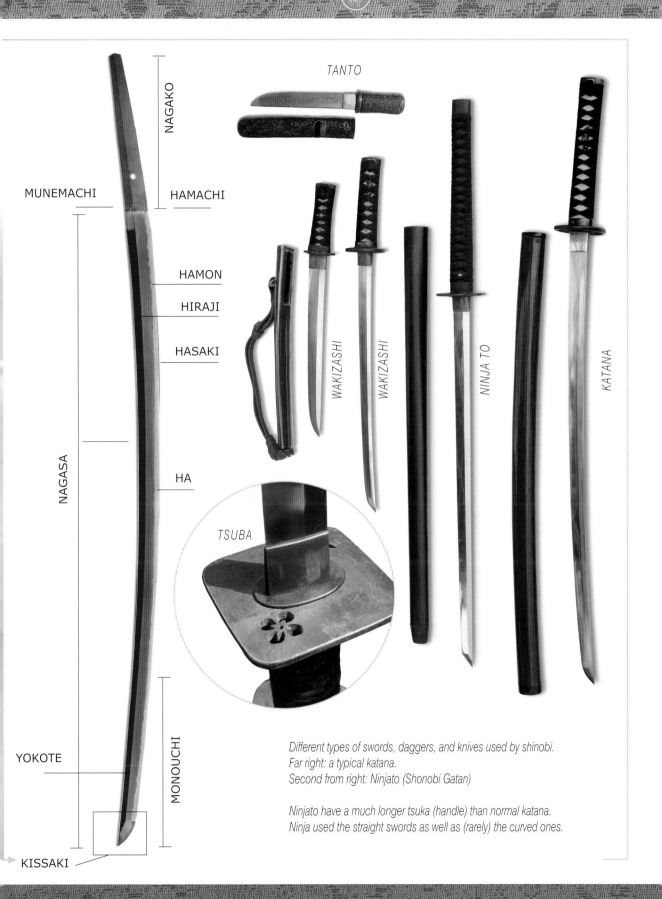

NAGAKO

MUNEMACHI

HAMACHI

HAMON

HIRAJI

HASAKI

NAGASA

HA

MONOUCHI

YOKOTE

KISSAKI

TANTO

WAKIZASHI

WAKIZASHI

NINJA TO

KATANA

TSUBA

Different types of swords, daggers, and knives used by shinobi.
Far right: a typical katana.
Second from right: Ninjato (Shonobi Gatan)

Ninjato have a much longer tsuka (handle) than normal katana.
Ninja used the straight swords as well as (rarely) the curved ones.

Ninja Shizumi Iai

The skill of pulling the sword out in confined spaces. While in the Hanza No Kamae position, a ninja controlling his surroundings pulls a ninjato out slowly.

While the left hand moves the saya backward, the right hand pulls the sword out.

For a moment, the ninja keeps the sword in one hand only, and then he grabs it with the second hand.

One should practice this movement in order to perform it fluidly and soundlessly.

DANGEROUS TECHNIQUE BEWARE

The left forearm pushes the saya close to the body. Another method is to keep both the end of saya and the tsuka in the left hand. These two methods are used to prevent the saya from knocking against the floor or on other objects, the sound of which might reveal the ninja's position.

Ninja Iai - Yoko Aruki

Pulling the sword out and moving to the side. This type of movement is useful when a ninja moves along a wall.

Pull the tsuka forward and up while moving Yoko Aruki. Kissaki is pointing forward. Now, you can hold the tsuka with one hand or you can perform another movement.

Ninja uses the Yoko Aruki movement, a walk to the side. He moves his left leg in front of the right. While walking to the side, Yoko Aruki, he calmly pulls his ninjato out.

Practice performing this movement noiselessly and fluidly.

Ninja To - Aruki 1

Presented is a different way of moving Aruki, such as when moving through bushes or thickets. The saya is used to remove obstacles; the weapon is ready to be used.

The sword is in front of the ninja, the blade facing down (opposite the regular way for carrying a weapon).

While stepping forward, the ninja brings the rear leg close to the front leg. Both feet are turned outward.

The ninja keeps the saya in front of him and checks his surroundings with it. If he identifies an obstacle, he can react. For example, he can use the saya to open and close shoji screens.

While moving, a ninja is ready to act, whether with an attack or counterattack.

Ninja To - Aruki 2

The Aruki walk: turning back in case of an attack from behind.

The saya is controlled by the left hand close to the tsuba. The elbow presses the sword against the body.

The ninja turns with his back straight and rotates on his body's axis.

After a 180-degree turn, the ninja gains the full capacity to attack or counterattack.

When the sword is pulled out, the blade faces outward.

Ninja To - Atypical Way of Pulling Out the Sword 1

This technique includes pulling a sword out with the left hand to mislead the opponent. In order to do it, the scabbard must be perfectly fitted to the obi (the belt). To place one's right hand on the handle was a sign of danger and a problem; showing the blade was a sign of open conflict and invited a fight. By pulling the sword out with the left hand, a ninja could strike the opponent's ribs with the end of the handle (tsuka gashira).

A sword in a saya. The left hand holds the tsuba and saya.

The hand moves in front of the tsuba. The ninja pulls the sword out quickly and smoothly, and simultaneously steps backward.

Ninja To- Atypical Way of Pulling Out the Sword 2

There are three situations in which a ninja would pull a sword out from behind his back or put the sword onto his back. The first situation is when a ninja would attach the sword behind his back while walking (rarely, because the other way was to attach it to his side). The second event was when the ninja attached the sword to his back while he was climbing or jumping through obstacles. The third case was when two shinobi were fighting one opponent. While one ninja remained in front of the opponent with his sword, the second ninja would move behind his partner's back and shift the sword to his back. The hidden ninja would then step out from behind his friend and launch a surprise attack against the opponent with Jodan Kiri.

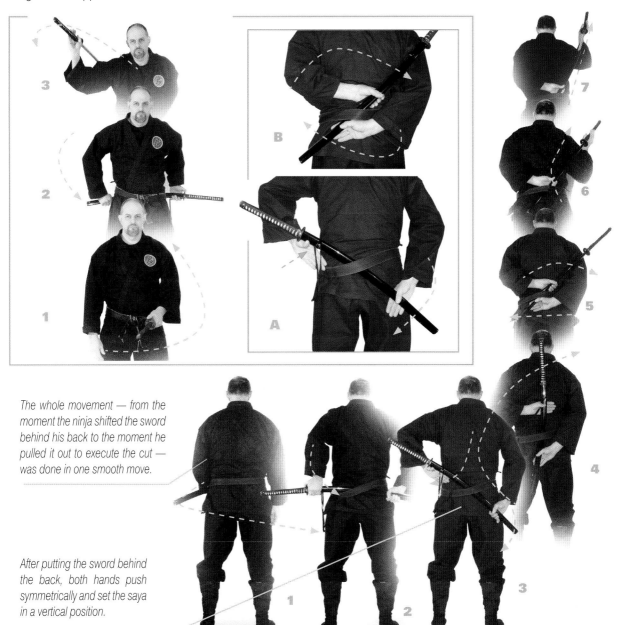

The whole movement — from the moment the ninja shifted the sword behind his back to the moment he pulled it out to execute the cut — was done in one smooth move.

After putting the sword behind the back, both hands push symmetrically and set the saya in a vertical position.

The Flowing Sword: A Training Form 1

Training for the fluid use of a sword while walking. Advanced students may use a real weapon for this practice. Training with a real sword completely changes the understanding of the movement, removing the sense of security and resulting in a more economic and realistic usage of the weapon. Using a standard katana of normal length improves the flow and enforces more extensive work with the body. Compared to katana, which was mostly used for cutting, ninjato were used mostly for stabbing.

The thumb on tsuba prevents the sword from sliding out of the scabbard. Also, if needed, the thumb can help to pull the sword out quicker.

Two cuts at hand level of the imagined opponent performed while walking. The ninja steps smoothly so as to avoid the opponent. Without stopping the ninja returns the sword to the saya.

DANGEROUS TECHNIQUE BEWARE

Putting the sword back into the scabbard can be performed close to the body, which stabilizes the weapon and protects its user from being cut. This also allows the weapon to always be ready for use. The whole form is performed while walking.

Pulling the Sword Back Into the Saya.

Two cuts at an imagined opponent, both done at hand level and performed while walking. The ninja steps smoothly so as to avoid the opponent. Without interrupting the walk, the ninja puts the sword back into the saya.

Flexible wrists and the use of the weapon's own weight are combined with the Aruki movement.

The Flowing Sword: A Training Form 2

Using the sword while walking in a 180-degree turn.

While turning, the ninja cuts through space parallel to the ground.

Two horizontal cuts, Do Giri, after a 180-degree turn, finishing with Jodan Giri. The flow finishes with a step back and the natural standing stance Shizen No Kamae.

A view from the above. A blade flows in circular and uninterrupted movement under the force of its own weight. A ninja holds a sword neither with tension nor with the force of muscle. He uses his whole body to lead the movement of the sword.

While raising the sword, Ninja keeps Kissaki, i.e., the tip of the sword, in front of him for protection until the moment of the cut.

During the second turn and the second cut, Do Giri, the tsuka should be held close to body for safety and for stabilizing the weapon.

Stopping an Attempt to Seize the Weapon

The method of preventing an opponent's attempt to seize the ninja's sword (ninjato, katana, wakizashi) with the use of the handle (tsuka). In traditional martial arts, when one lost his own weapon, an attempt was made to get the opponent's weapon. The presented technique is an example of how to prevent an enemy from "disarming" you and how to overpower the opponent without hurting him.

At the moment the opponent reaches for tori's sword handle and tries to pull the sword out, the ninja steps forward and pulls the saya, the scabbard, in the direction of the opponent's movement.

As a result, the sword is pushed back into the scabbard. Tori's left thumb holds the tsuba and pushes the sword up. With his right hand, tori grabs the right elbow of his opponent, who is still holding the handle. Tori applies the lock.

Continuing the technique as seen from a different angle.

Having his arm on the handle and the ninja's hand on his elbow, the opponent has his arm painfully locked. When the ninja pushes him forward, the opponent is forced to roll to avoid falling onto his head.

Step forward to shorten the distance, thus immobilizing the opponent in the position of having his hand on the sword handle.

DANGEROUS TECHNIQUE BEWARE

From the moment the opponent has his arm locked, both before and after the roll, Tori has him under complete control. A ninja can then finish his technique with a chosen ending.

Attack Without Warning

A form from Takagi Yoshin Ryu. This method was used by double agents who, under cover, snuck into a castle and gained the trust of the people inside.

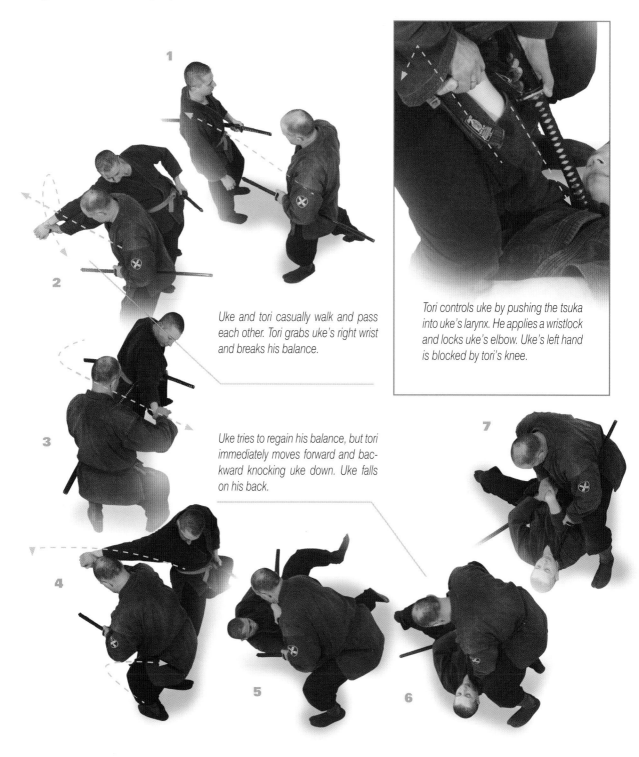

Uke and tori casually walk and pass each other. Tori grabs uke's right wrist and breaks his balance.

Tori controls uke by pushing the tsuka into uke's larynx. He applies a wristlock and locks uke's elbow. Uke's left hand is blocked by tori's knee.

Uke tries to regain his balance, but tori immediately moves forward and backward knocking uke down. Uke falls on his back.

The same technique as seen from a different angle.

Control over the opponent is achieved by a wristlock, an elbow lock, and applying pressure on the larynx with the tsuka.

Tori and uke pass each other casually. Tori grabs uke's wrist and breaks uke's balance.

Uke tries to regain his balance, but tori immediately moves forward and backward knocking uke down. Uke falls on his back.

DANGEROUS TECHNIQUE BEWARE

Happo Gakure No Kamae

"Look straight to his eyes so you will not miss a moment. This may be the last." Strategy from Togakure Ryu Ninpo.

Uke tries to pull his katana from the saya to attack tori. Tori stays in the open position Happo Gakure No Kamae. Anticipating uke's movement, tori immediately shortens the distance between him and uke.

Tori's left hand blocks the opponent's movement and stops uke's right hand from pulling the sword out. Tori applies Boshi Ken, a thumb strike at the sensitive point under uke's nose. The point's name is Jinchu (the center of humanity).

Tori steps on the opponent's right foot with his left foot. The opponent can neither move nor change position.

Tori kneels and throws uke. Uke falls on his back. Tori controls uke with the saya, then with the sword blade as well. The opponent is unable to move or to mount an counterattack due the position of the saya and the sword.

1

2

11

10

Tori gains control by grabbing the handle and stepping on the opponent's foot. The opponent can neither escape nor change the position of his body.

9

8

6

7

Tori grabs the tsuka and controls the opponent's right foot. He presses the tsuka against the opponent's chest. With two circular movements tori applies two locks: Omote Gyaku (the twisting wristlock) with his left hand and Ura Onikudaki (the elbow lock) with the use of the tsuba.

Ninjato: Saya

The unusual use of a sword. Using a sword in a surprising way often helped a ninja defeat a confused opponent. Below, the saya and sageo (that is, a scabbard and a rope that was used to tie the weapon to the belt) are used as a catapult and a bullet. The opponent's eyes or solar plexus was the usual target for this kind of attack.

Tori holds the sageo and saya in a way that the opponent cannot recognize his intensions.

Tori "fires" the saya from the sageo, which is under tension and thus used as a catapult. The saya doesn't cause serious damage but simply confuses the opponent.

Tori closes the distance by stepping forward. From this distance, he applies a sword cut from below. Depending on the opponent's reaction to the saya being fired at him, the tori's cut targets the opponent's forearms, trunk, or neck.

The same technique as seen from a different angle.

A natural position encourages the opponent to attack with a straight cut from above. The opponent's hand goes up, and he is open to any attack.

If the opponent is wearing armor or a thick winter gi, the saya attack is directed to the face (eyes, nose).

After tori executes his cut from below, which is targeted at the opponent's forearms, wrists, or torso, he will frequently finish the technique with a cut from above.

DANGEROUS TECHNIQUE BEWARE

The Hidden Weapon

The use of a hidden weapon. In this case, the hidden weapon is a senban shuriken, widely used by ninjas. The ninja warriors frequently used Shurikenjutsu to distract opponents, to perform a surprise attack, or as a means to disappear into the darkness.

Tori surprises uke by throwing the shuriken at uke's face. Tori hid the shuriken in his right hand, which was resting on the handle of his weapon.

The attacker loses his orientation. When he lowers his weapon, tori uses the aruki walking movement to step to the left, placing his ninjato on the opponent's wrists.

One of the principles of Togakure Ryu Ninpo was to not kill an enemy if possible. Getting into a fight was treated as an avoidable way of jeopardizing one's life. Further, a fight meant putting at risk the mission being conducted. The death of an enemy aroused the desire for revenge among the dead person's relatives. Death attracted unnecessary troubles.

Tori surprises the attacker by throwing a shuriken at his face. The shuriken is hidden in tori's right hand resting on the sword's handle.

DANGEROUS TECHNIQUE BEWARE

Tori immediately moves and adjusts the level of control over uke, placing the sword at uke's throat. Tori moves the sword up and then down, forcing the opponent to lie on his back.

5

6

7

The Reverse Blade

Keeping the sword with the blade facing the opponent's face is typical for the Kukishinden Ryu Happo Bikenjutsu.

The sitting stance, Seiza. Tori is focused; he can anticipate the opponent, Zanshin. Because tori expects the opponent to attack with his left hand, tori turns his sword upside down in the saya. His thumb rests on the tsuba. His thumb pushes the sword out and initiates the cut.

Tori's right hand grabs the sword's handle inversely: underneath and with the thumb facing outward. From the kneeling position, tori moves his right knee forward and lifts it dynamically, placing his right foot flat on the ground.

The cut targets the opponent's face and should be performed before the opponent's sword begins its downward trajectory. This technique, the first in a series, is conducted with the right hand, while the left hand rests on the hip and keeps the saya close to the body.

The same technique as seen from a different angle.

Tori's right hand grabs the sword's handle inversely: underneath and with the thumb facing outward. From the kneeling position, tori moves his right knee forward and lifts it dynamically, placing his right foot flat on the ground.

Tori anticipates the opponent's movement, lifting his sword up with the blade facing out into the open space in front of uke. This movement blocks uke's movement. This technique, the first in a series, is conducted with the right hand, while the tori's left hand rests on the hip and keeps the saya close to the body. Tori thrusts the sword's blade at uke's throat. During this move, tori ensures that his sword blocks uke's hand.

DANGEROUS TECHNIQUE BEWARE

The finishing cut in the series is applied from above downward at the opponent, who is off balance. The cut is done at the same time as the forward step of the right foot.

Counterattack with Taihenjutsu

As presented below, the way of moving with ninjato will surprise the opponent, who expects a confrontation. The presented movement allows shinobi to avoid engaging in a fight.

Initially, tori keeps his guard up. Then he opens the guard and shifts his balance slightly forward. He lowers his katana to his right knee. Uke attacks with Jodan Giri, a cut to the head.

Tori moves to the right while holding his weapon with only one hand. Tori executes a front roll, Zen Po Kai Ten Katate, and with a wide arc cuts the back of uke's knee.

Tori moves to the right while holding his weapon with only one hand. Tori executes a front roll, Zen Po Kai Ten Katate, and with a wide arc cuts the back of uke's knee.

DANGEROUS TECHNIQUE BEWARE

1

2

3

4

5

6

7

After the cut, tori assumes a position that enables him to continue the confrontation. Zanshin stance (focus and observation).

Shortening the Distance: Bo Against Shinobito

The ability to shorten the distance when one possesses a weapon that is shorter than the opponent's weapon is a difficult, yet extremely important skill. It is often a matter of life or death. The ability could also be used in modern circumstances to defend against someone with a large and dangerous object.

Tori steps back with his left leg and shifts his sword behind him.

Uke immediately tries to strike Toki Uchi from the left with his bo at tori's leg. But tori changes his position and blocks the strike with the tip of his katana.

Uke strikes Kasumi Uchi to tori's head. Tori uses this moment to close the distance to his opponent.

Tori places the blade of his sword on the top of the opponent's bo, blocking uke's fingers and his neck. Tori pushes the bo and manages to move forward.

The stick — bo — blocks the katana, so it's locked on the opponent's neck. The opponent's body prevents him from moving or attempting any defensive techniques.

DANGEROUS TECHNIQUE BEWARE

Tori unexpectedly changes the pace of movement and grabs the bo. He applies a dangerous lock to the uke's neck with the blade of the sword. Uke, being caught, allows tori to lead him. Tori pushes uke to the ground and gains total control over uke.

Staff Weaponry

Hanbo
Jo
Bo

Bo - Furi Gata

A flow movement with bo in front and behind the body. This form teaches both how to hold a bo steady in your hands and how to move smoothly with a bo, skills that are necessary during a fight. While moving the bo in front of his body, the tori should create a triangle that protects himself from an attack. Practicing with the bo develops the ability to use any type of wooden weapon. It is an introduction and foundation to learning how to use a yari (spear) and naginata.

Bō (roku-shaku-bō) literally means stick. It has a length of 6 shaku, where one shaku is 12 inches (30.3 cm). Its length depends on a user's height and is usually about 70 inches (180 cm). A bo is made from wood or bamboo; they are rarely made from metal.

During movement, the bo should always be at such an angle with the body so as to protect the user from attack.

In order to execute smooth movements with a bo, one must integrate the movement of the bo with the movement of the body. While in motion, the stick should at least be held with all the fingers of one hand; without doing so, the user may lose the bo.

An unusual handling of the bo behind one's back. Tori turns around at the same time.

Bo (2)

A series of movements that includes two horizontal strikes and shifting the bo behind the back. This may lead to a vertical strike.

One's grip on the bo determines the distance (range of the bo's strike), as well as the strength, of the applied technique.

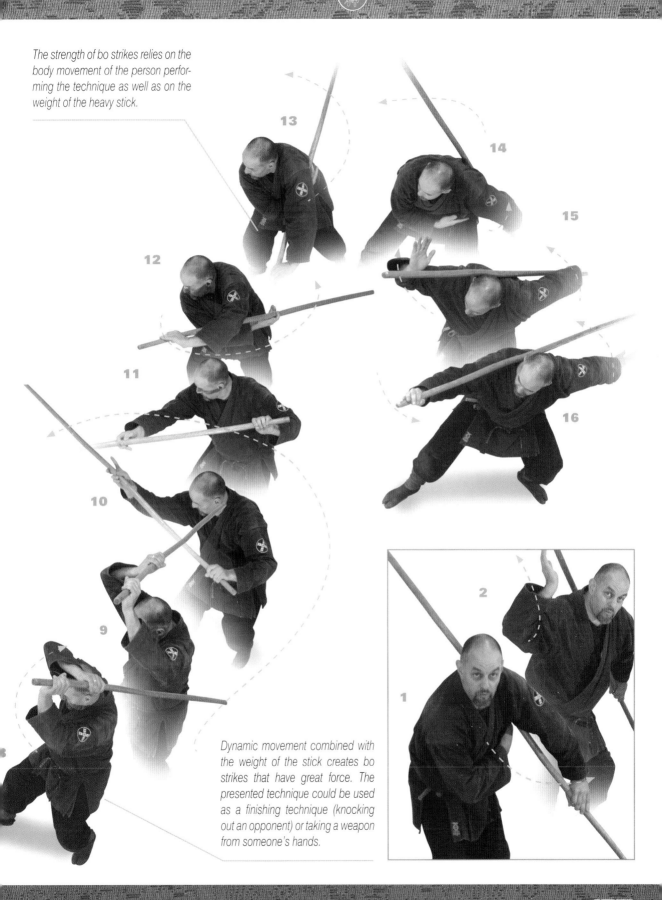

The strength of bo strikes relies on the body movement of the person performing the technique as well as on the weight of the heavy stick.

13

14

15

12

11

16

10

9

2

1

Dynamic movement combined with the weight of the stick creates bo strikes that have great force. The presented technique could be used as a finishing technique (knocking out an opponent) or taking a weapon from someone's hands.

Bo (3)

The combination of using a bo with other objects. Ninja moves with the bo targeted at the opponent. Tori kicks an object up from the ground to distract the opponent.

Ninja looks directly at the opponent and keeps his weapon targeted at the opponent. The opponent doesn't pay attention to his surroundings because he expects danger from only one direction.

The ninja performing the technique kicks the object up from the ground. The object distracts the opponent for a moment. This exposes him to further techniques from the ninja: a stab with the bo, for example.

These pictures show walking with the bo in the open position, kicking the object up from the ground, and a horizontal strike Kasumi Uchi to the opponent's head.

During the movement, the person performing the technique does not look at the object on the ground. He looks at the opponent the whole time.

Seigan no Kamae stance. Tori holds the bo in his right hand at belt level. His left hand holds the bo with elbow bent close to his body. The bo is targeted at the opponent.

The series may be finished with Tsuki, which is a forward thrust of the bo's tip.

Bo (4)

Picking the bo up from the ground without bending or losing eye contact with the target.

When picked up, the bo may be used in any given technique.

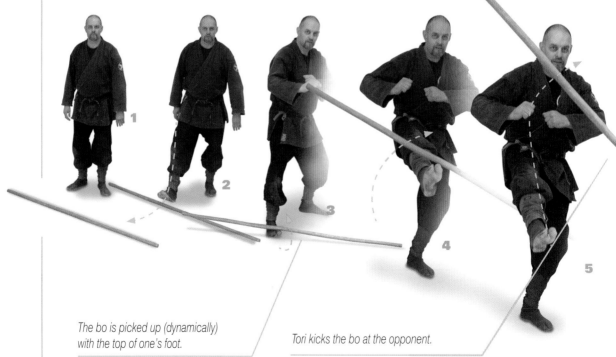

The bo is picked up (dynamically) with the top of one's foot.

Tori kicks the bo at the opponent.

The opponent is hit by bo and loses full control over the situation. He is open to further attack.

Without warning, tori may kick the bo at the opponent.

Immediately after attacking with a bo, tori can perform any other technique.

DANGEROUS TECHNIQUE BEWARE

Jō (1)

A jo is a wooden stick, usually about 50 inches (128 cm) long, often of a length adjusted to the user's height. However, the jo is always longer than a katana. In the past, the jo was used to defend against the katana, wakizashi, and tanto.

Some jo techniques are similar to, or the same as, techniques used from schools that used short spears.

Tori stands sideway towards the uke. Tori maintains the Ichimonji no Kamae stance. Uke attacks Jodan Giri, a cut from above tori's head.

1

2

3

4

5

A strike to the opponent's open guard, aimed at stopping the attack, requires exquisite timing from tori.

Tsuki to the throat was commonly used due to the open space existing in traditional armor at this level of the body.

Tori changes his position. He strikes from beneath to the opponent's open guard and then immediately to the opponent's left hand. Tori finishes with Tsuki to uke's throat.

DANGEROUS TECHNIQUE BEWARE

Jō (2)

This technique can also be used with a bo (a wooden stick approximately 70 inches [180 cm] long) or with a yari (a spear).

Tori stays in the open stance Kyohen no Kamae. His weapon (in this case a jo) is hidden behind his back so the opponent is unsure what tori has.

Uke tries to close the distance and cut diagonally from above, Migi Kesa Giri, to tori's head.

Tori can shift the jo by moving it from hand to hand behind his back. Then he attacks from above, Men Uchi. Tori's gaze must be focused in front of him. Men Uchi can be performed with one or both hands on the jo.

When the opponent tries to attack again, tori pulls the jo from behind his back and strikes from above at uke's hands on the sword.

With jo, tori controls uke's hands, which are holding the sword. Tori pushes uke's hands down and kick uke's forearm at elbow level.

Hanbo

The technique with a hanbo, a short stick, is used to incapacitate an attacker who uses a short sword.

The hanbo is a stick about 35 inches (90 cm) long. It should be the same length as the distance from the user's belly button to the ground. The stick's length is similar to that of everyday objects such as an umbrella, a pipe from a vacuum cleaner, etc. The stick can be used as a walking stick. In the past, some would place a dagger or even a sword inside a hanbo. This would transform the hanbo into shikomibuki, which is an insidious type of weapon.

Tori stays in the stance Munen Muso no Kamae (a position of no expectations and no thoughts). Uke uses a wakizashi. Uke moves forward and applies Tsuki to the Chudan level.

In defense, tori moves back to open the distance. Tori strikes with his hanbo to uke's weapon or arm. Next, tori strikes to the neck or head with Yokomen.

Tori holds the hanbo with the thumb directed towards the end of the stick closer to him and performs figure-eight like movements with it.

DANGEROUS TECHNIQUE BEWARE

Tori closes the distance and applies a chocking lock by pressing his elbow against uke's throat on one side while pressing the hanbo against uke's neck on the other side. The hanbo crushes the vertebrae.

Tori escapes from the line of attack (moving to the right and forward) as a defense against a sword attack.

Tori grabs the hanbo with both hands and strongly strikes at the opponent's wrist. The opponent loses his weapon.

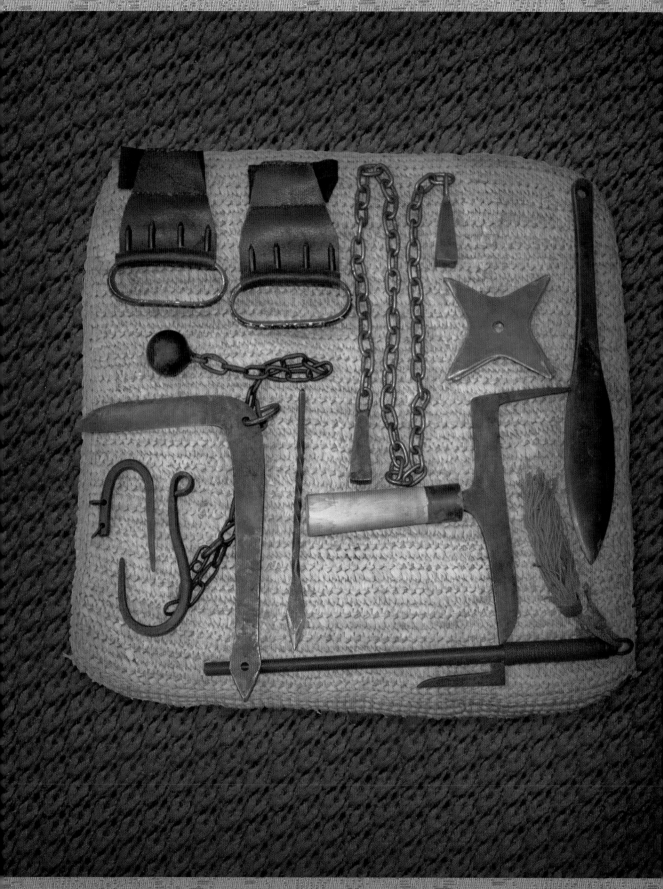

Ningu:

Kyoketsu
Shuko
Kunai

Shuriken

Jitte

Ningu is a word generally used to describe all kinds of tools used by ninja warriors. There is much discussion and misconception about the tools used by a ninja. Some people who love the dressed-in--black warriors seen in Hollywood movies are unaware that ninjas did not actually create the weapons so widely associated with them. Furthermore, regular samurai warriors used the same weapons as well. A typical subject of such misconception is the shuriken. It was a small object that took various shapes; a warrior usually threw it at an opponent's face. Shurikenjutsu was a part of the training system in many martial arts schools where samurai practiced their skills. Shinobi warriors also used this weapon; some shapes of shuriken can be exclusively linked to ninja schools.

While ninjas used weapons that were generally available, it's important to mention at this point that very often they used such weapons in their own way: they applied their own methods and combat strategies.

Kyoketsu, kunai, shuko, and ashiko were typical for ninjas.

Kyoketsu Shogei (1)

This weapon is considered to be a type of ningu (ninja equipment). It was a typical shinobi weapon (as opposed to the shuriken, which was also employed by samurai). The kyoketsu is a brilliant tool with many characteristics that are very useful during combat, climbing, and tying up an opponent. It combined many functions. In a ninja's hands it was a multifunctional tool as well as a deadly weapon. The tool would have two double-edged blades, a long rope measuring 8-10 feet (2.5-3 meters) that would have been made from the hair of a horse or woman, and a metal ring. The blades were used to wound an opponent, the ring was used for strikes in various vital points, and the rope was used to bind an opponent using Hayanawa techniques.

Tori performs wide figure-eight-like movements in front of himself. He catches the rope and the metal ring under his foot.

He throws the ring in front of him. After that, he leads the ring between and behind his legs, causing the ring to lose its momentum.

Tori moves the kyoketsu in a figure-eight-like movement. At the same time he moves around his own axis.

Tori finishes the technique with a diagonal throw forward and upwards. The blades are kept close to the body.

Kyoketsu Shogei (2)

At the beginning of a fight, kyoketsu shogei is used as a long-range weapon. A technique in which one can entwine an opponent's leg or neck with rope thus qualifies kyoketsu shoge as a "flexible" weapon, similar to a chain. It can be very dangerous when used by beginners. To use the tool for one's advantage, one must absolutely control the tool; otherwise, the tool can be dangerous for the person using it.

The metal ring thrown from a distance can unpleasantly surprise an opponent. In the picture, the person using the kyoketsu shogei employs it from above his head.

The rope wraps around the opponent's leg. With a strong jolt tori trips up the opponent.

The metal ring prevents the rope from sliding off the leg.

Tori swings the ring above his head in a circular trajectory and then throws it. The rope wraps around uke's neck.

DANGEROUS TECHNIQUE BEWARE

Metal rings anchor the rope around the opponent's neck.

The success of this technique depends on the Taijutsu skills possessed by tori, i.e., the ability to take the opponent's balance with a minimum force involved in the technique.

Kyoketsu Shogei (3)

The techniques presented below are for striking the opponent's head, trunk, or arms with the metal ring as well as a technique that enables tori to pull the opponent down. Tori throws the kyoketsu shogei at the opponent's guard. The ring targets the space between the opponent's arms. The attacker with a sword now has metal ring hanging on his arm. It definitely causes problems for the swordsman, as there is a ninja in front of him just waiting for a mistake. The attacker does not know whether he should change his grip on his sword, cut the rope between the ring and ninja, or just wait for the ninja's next move. For a ninja it was sometimes enough just to throw a kyoketsu shogei at a man with a sword. The object would hit the hand holding the katana, and the fight was over.

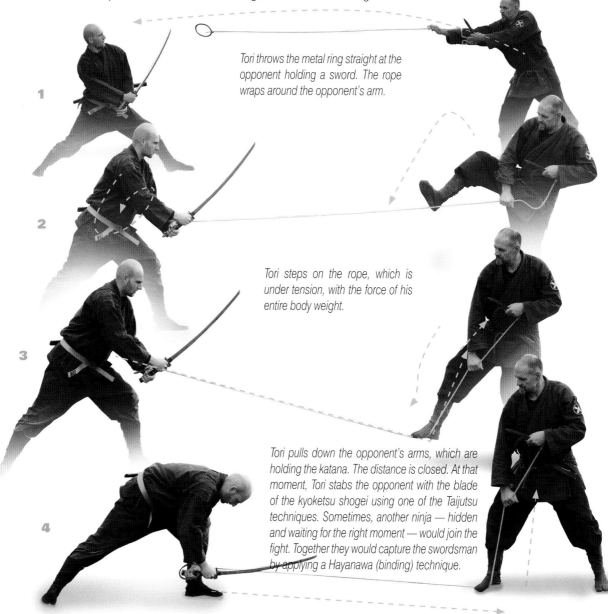

1

2

3

4

Tori throws the metal ring straight at the opponent holding a sword. The rope wraps around the opponent's arm.

Tori steps on the rope, which is under tension, with the force of his entire body weight.

Tori pulls down the opponent's arms, which are holding the katana. The distance is closed. At that moment, Tori stabs the opponent with the blade of the kyoketsu shogei using one of the Taijutsu techniques. Sometimes, another ninja — hidden and waiting for the right moment — would join the fight. Together they would capture the swordsman by applying a Hayanawa (binding) technique.

2

3

The Ichiminji position: a ring on the ground by the foot; the blade is in the left hand and faces forward.

The ring thrown at a chosen target: head, arms, or legs.

The ninja's right hand directs the metal ring to the chosen target.

The technique of throwing the ring from the foot.

DANGEROUS TECHNIQUE BEWARE

Shuriken

This small steel weapon was frequently used by shinobi warriors. In their hands it became quite an efficient weapon. A few types of shurikan can be distinguished:
- straight shurikan;
- in the shape of star, cross or disc;
- special shurikan.

Shurikan techniques were taught in many martial arts schools. Even today students practice Shurikenjutsu in the Bujinkan and in some samurai schools. Throws are executed from almost every kind of position: lying on the ground, after turning around, from the hip, and backwards.

Traditionally, shuriken techniques were used in combat in fights at a mid-length distance. The weapon was most efficient when thrown from a distance of 7-10 feet (2-3 meters). It was usually thrown at the opponent's head and neck and would wound and scare the opponent.

In modern circumstances the shuriken techniques could be used for self-defense. We can throw objects that are within reach and match these categories:
- straight: pen, fork, knife, spoon, stick, etc.;
- in the shape of star, cross, or disc: ashtray, saucer, plate, etc.;
- special ones: book, glass, or any other object.

Shuriken of all designs make effective and dangerous weapons in close-in fighting.

Various types of steel shurikens. Different shapes and forms were characteristic for particular regions and areas of Japan. Based on shape, it is therefore possible to discover the origins of particular shuriken.

The senbam shuriken is also known as the "Throwing Star" and "Ninja Death Star." This shuriken is square shaped, with grooves on the side and a square-shaped hole in the middle. Shuriken was used in Kukishin schools. Techniques with the senbam shuriken were secret.

The method of throwing bo shuriken: the shuri-ken is hidden in the ninja's left-hand sleeve. The shuriken is thrown with the right hand. Tori starts the throw from the right side and at the level of his head. After throwing it, the ninja attacks by apply-ing a Tsuki thrust with ninjato.

The method of holding bo shuriken in the hand for a forward throw: the thumb holds the shank while blade is between fingers.

Manriki Kusari (1)

Kusarijutsu, the art of the chain, includes strikes (Atemi) targeted at particular points, thrusts (Tsuki), attacks targeted at eyes (Metsubushi), blocks (Uke), sparring (Uke nagashi), tying (Karami), controlling (Osae), choking (Shime), and binding (Hobaku).

The Hiken Uchi technique of throwing the chain forward and horizontally is called "Strike of the Flying Fist." The picture shows the technique performed while walking: the chain is thrown as the right leg moves forward.

The picture shows the technique performed from the natural standing stance, Shizen no Kamae. The ninja throws the chain using the power coming from his hips. The chain is hidden in the ninja's hand, which allows him to completely surprise the opponent.

DANGEROUS TECHNIQUE BEWARE

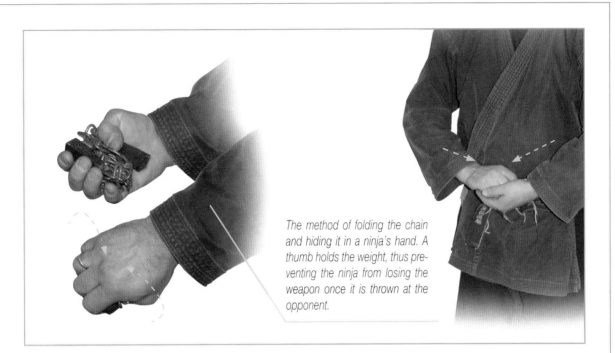

The method of folding the chain and hiding it in a ninja's hand. A thumb holds the weight, thus preventing the ninja from losing the weapon once it is thrown at the opponent.

Tsuki, a straight strike and thrust to Matsu Kaze, the sensitive atemi point located below the collarbone.

The Atemi In strike to the cheekbone using a steel weight.

Manriki Kusari (2)

Furiuchiwaza: the technique of swinging a chain horizontally, vertically, or diagonally when attacking.

Swinging the chain horizontally, vertically, or diagonally with one hand. The free hand is kept close to the body for safety reasons.

The swinging movement gets its power from the movement of the whole body. The method of suppressing the move is to wrap the chain around one's waist above the hips.

A well-executed movement with great flow enables the ninja to move to the next technique in the chosen direction.

The method of suppressing the move is to wrap the chain around the ninja's waist above the hips.

1

2

3

4

5

9

8

Depending on the ninja's needs, a strike with the metal weight could be targeted directly at a palm (metacarpus) or at a palm after wrapping around the hand.

DANGEROUS TECHNIQUE BEWARE

Kakushi Kusarigama

Kusarigama was a small, useful, and effective weapon that could be hidden in a kimono. The weapon was used to block a sword blade, to immobilize the opponent's hand on a sword handle, to execute cuts with the sickle, to strike and thrust with the sharp handle, as well as to choke or strike with the round weight at the end of the chain.

Tori opens his position, thus encouraging uke to execute a cut from above. Uke attacks Jodan Kiri to the head.

1

2

3

Tori steps aside (Aruki) to the left; he blocks uke's hand with the sickle. Pushing at the sickle, tori forces uke to shift his weight to his back leg. Tori strikes uke's left palm with the iron weight. Uke releases the weapon from his left hand.

4

5

Tori steps aside (Aruki) to the left; he blocks uke's hand with the sickle. Pushing at the sickle, tori forces uke to shift his weigh to his back leg. Tori strikes uke's left palm with the iron weight. Uke releases the weapon from his left hand.

Tori moves behind uke and sets the sickle at uke's throat. Using a broad motion, tori moves the chain behind uke's head. From behind uke's back, tori applies a choking technique from the Ichimonji position. The off-balance uke is under tori's control.

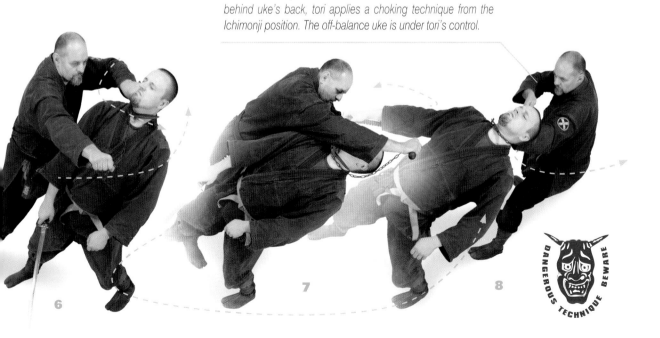

DANGEROUS TECHNIQUE BEWARE

Jutte (Juttejutsu 1)

This weapon is associated with police from the Edo period (1603-1868). There were many kinds of jutte. The length of the weapon ranged from 9 inches to 25 inches (25 cm to 64 cm). During the Edo period, police used juttes that ranged from 35 inches to 40 inches (90-101 cm). The jutte was used for intercepting katanas; for strikes, thrusts, and chokes; and for locks applied to wrists, elbows, and fingers.

A jutte (jitte) is comprised of a blunt basic steel shaft and hook with a sharp tip attached to it. A colorful fringe was often attached to the handle.

Tori stays in open position thus encouraging uke to attack. Uke attacks with Jodan Giri from above. Tori moves to the left and blocks uke's left hand. At the same time he uses the jutte to hook the uke's sword. Tori uses his weight to push the opponent and to gain control of the opponent's weapon.

When uke shifts his weight to his back leg, tori immediately grabs uke's left hand. Tori simultaneously pushes the katana down and towards him, pulls uke towards him, and in a circular movement moves to the right.

Tori applies a scissor lock on uke's neck by using the jutte and the sword blade. This is possible, as tori had previously taken his opponent's balance.

Tori moves around and forces uke to the ground, whereupon tori gains full control.

The blades of the jutte and the sword create scissors on uke's neck, choking him.

DANGEROUS TECHNIQUE BEWARE

Jutte (Juttejutsu 2)

The jutte can be understood as an extension of the hand. Strikes with a metal rod are stronger than simple Koppo Jutsu strikes. Pressing Kyusho points with a metal pole is more effective then simply pressing those points with fingers. The hook attached to the rod can wound and tear skin, yet one can also use it to break fingers or apply small but very effective locks. The jutte was usually hidden in a person's sleeve, attached behind the person's back to the belt, or inserted in a person's leggings. During a fight, it was often an unpleasant surprise for the opponent.

Tori has a jutte hidden in his left sleeve. Uke attacks Fudo Ken Jodan. Tori moves slightly to the right. He takes a jutte out of his sleeve and seizes uke's hand (Uke Nagashi). He places the jutte on uke's arm.

Tori moves uke's arm back and outward. Uke is off balance. Tori moves uke's wrist toward his chest. At the same time, he strikes uke's neck with the jutte.

Moving uke's hand back and outward takes uke's balance. Tori simultaneously strikes uke's neck with the jutte.

1

2

3

Again, tori moves uke's arm outward. Tori moves to the left and lowers his weapon to uke's leg. Tori strikes the back of uke's knee with a wide, circular movement.

6

7

8

Again, tori moves uke's arm outward. Tori moves to the left and lowers the weapon. Tori strikes the back of uke's knee with a wide, circular movement.

DANGEROUS TECHNIQUE BEWARE

Shuko (Cat Hand 1)

The defense against a sword cut to the head: a technique from Togakure Ryu Ninpo.

The shuko is a metal claw worn on the hand. Similar claws, called ashiko, were also worn on the legs. The claws were used at close distances for tearing and stabbing an opponent, for blocking a sword cut using the small metal band that was wrapped around the hand, for parrying a sword attack, or for disarming an opponent by hitting his hand with a fist armed with a metal band. The metal claws had a definite psychological effect on an opponent. The wounds caused by the claw could be very dangerous or even deadly.

Uke attacks tori's head with Jodan Giri. Tori moves to the right and hooks uke's hand with the sword.

Tori seizes the sword handle from underneath with his right hand. His left hand grabs the opponent's second hand from the top. Tori lowers his body and pulls the katana out of uke's hands and leads the blade towards the opponent's torso.

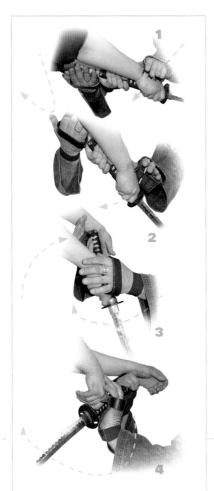

A similar situation. Tori holds the opponent's wrist with the shuko while with his right elbow he knocks the opponent's hand from the handle of the sword.

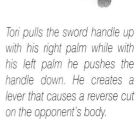

Tori pulls the sword handle up with his right palm while with his left palm he pushes the handle down. He creates a lever that causes a reverse cut on the opponent's body.

Shuko (Cat Hand 2)

The defense against Migi Do Giri (a horizontal sword cut from the right side) is a technique from Togakure Ryu Ninpo.

A martial art called Shukojutsu used the shuko's counterpart, which were worn on the legs and were called ashiko. Fighting with these tools at close range, a ninja could painfully injure the opponent by tearing and stabbing him. A popular target for ninjas was the inside of the thigh.

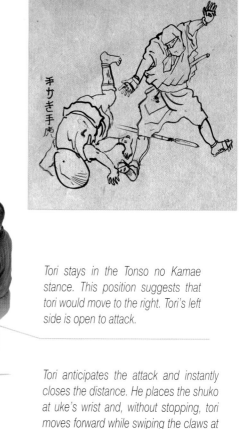

Tori stays in the Tonso no Kamae stance. This position suggests that tori would move to the right. Tori's left side is open to attack.

Tori anticipates the attack and instantly closes the distance. He places the shuko at uke's wrist and, without stopping, tori moves forward while swiping the claws at uke's face.

1

2

3

4

5

All moves must be performed in a flow. There is no break between steps.

DANGEROUS TECHNIQUE BEWARE

Tori pivots to the right. With his right elbow and right leg tori controls uke. Tori moves behind uke and, controlling his whole body with two hands, pulls uke down.

Kunai

A kunai was used in close-range combat to apply strikes and thrusts even though its tip wasn't sharp.

A kunai can serve as an example of a regular object that in the experienced and skilled hands of a ninja could become a dangerous weapon.

Tori stays in an open position. The kunai is hidden behind tori's leg. The opponent attacks Migi Kesa Giri to the left side of tori's head. Tori reacts rapidly and does not allow uke to complete the attack. Tori counterattacks by using the fact that uke left his hands up.

Tori moves forward and stops the attack. He points the kunai at the uke. Tori moves to the left with the intention of gaining control over uke's right hand. Tori takes control of uke's elbow and strikes the crook of uke's arm with the edge of the kunai.

Tori controls uke's elbow and strikes uke's arm with the kunai. Tori also strikes uke's wrist and knocks the weapon out of uke's hands.

The kunai is a multi-purpose metal tool used for climbing stone walls or digging. At the end of the handle of the kunai, there was a ring for attaching a rope. A ninja might have found this useful during a nighttime mission. A kunai was made in different sizes. Daikunai or great kunai ranged from 13-19 inches (35-48 cm); Shokunai, a small kunai, was about 7 inches (18 cm) long.

DANGEROUS TECHNIQUE BEWARE

Tori knocks the weapon out of uke's hand. He controls uke with the kunai and then applies the Genseki Nage lock.

A kunai was used in close-distance combat for striking and thrusting at the opponent, although the tip of a kunai wasn't necessary sharp.

Tori opens the opponent's position with a circular hand movement. He applies the elbow lock Genseki Nage while pushing the kunai against uke's throat.

Tori pulls uke to the ground using the control he gained through the lock and the kunai. Tori leads uke towards his own sword on the ground, which adds an additional aspect of control.

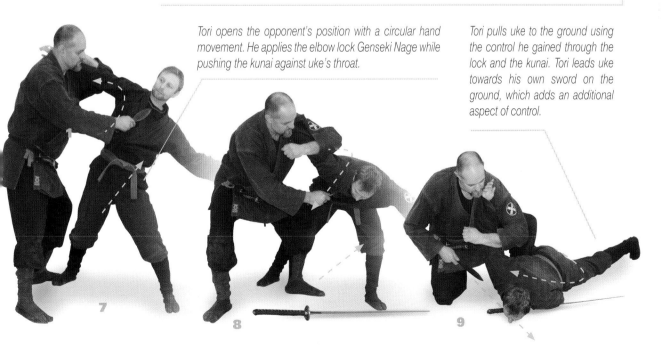

Other Objects as Combat Tools

Many everyday items can be used as tools for combat. In general, objects can be divided into the following categories:

– long and fixed, for example: a stick, umbrella, broom, shovel, pen, fork, and book. They are the equivalents of a katana, bamboo, tanto, bo shuriken, jo, bo, and tassen (fan).

– long and flexible, for example: a robe, belt, scarf, leash, and chain. They are the equivalents of a sageo, manriki, kusari, etc.

– round and hard: stone, ashtray, and jug. They are the equivalents of star-shaped shuriken, disc-shaped shuriken, etc.

– in granular or fluid form: sand, pepper, salt, baking soda, coins, water, etc. They are the equivalents of metsubushi, a blinding powder.

Tori stays in an open, receiving position. The opponent passes by but suddenly grabs tori by the lapels.

Tori shifts his body weight, and, at the same time, steps on the soft part of a rake. With the rake handle he pushes uke's elbow.

Tori changes his grip on the rake. His left hand grabs the rake beneath uke's hand; at the same time, tori steps backward with his right foot.

Tori lowers his position and strikes at uke's genitals.

DANGEROUS TECHNIQUE BEWARE

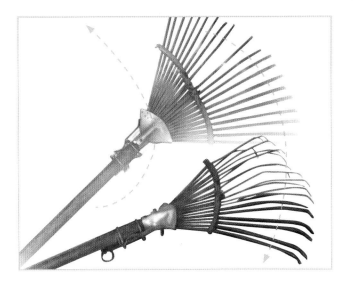

Tori steps forward and attacks the side of uke's head.

7

6

5

Tori moves up the body with the rake's metal fingers. He points the rake at uke's eyes

Tori stays in an open, receiving position. The opponent approaches tori and grabs tori's top. Tori shifts his body weight and steps on the soft part of the rake. With the rake handle he pushes uke's elbow.

Incapacitation: a Street Fight

The application of self-defense techniques for immobilizing is presented in modern circumstances with the use of a sport coat or jacket. It is an example of the use of modern clothing belonging either to the attacker or the person performing the techniques. Clothing — along with belts, robes, etc. — belongs to the category of flexible weapons. The different parts of clothing are perfect tools that can be used for different purposes such as for binding, immobilizing, applying pins and locks, choking, or blocking an opponent's view. Various types of shoes are useful for different kinds of kicks. The jacket sleeve can be used for binding and immobilizing. Hats and gloves are perfect for throwing at an opponent's eyes for the purposes of distraction.

Uke grabs tori by his top. Tori steps back and opens uke's grip by striking from under the opponent's arm.

Tori moves forward towards uke and strikes uke's neck. Tori grabs uke's jacket with both hands.

DANGEROUS TECHNIQUE BEWARE

Tori pushes uke down, strikes uke's face with his head, and splits uke's jacket in half. Tori pulls uke's jacket down.

Another way of moving behind the opponent. Tori strikes uke with his forearm, which blocks uke's view. Tori moves behind uke.

While behind uke's back, tori controls uke's jacket with his left hand while covering uke's eyes, Shako Ken, with his right hand. Tori pulls uke to the ground. Tori maintains control over uke. Uke stretches his own arms and his own jacket immobilizes him.

Tori moves around uke and pushes uke with his shoulders. Tori controls uke.

Published by Tuttle Publishing, an imprint of Periplus Editions
(HK) Ltd.

www.tuttlepublishing.com

Copyright © 2013 Marian Winiecki

ISBN: 978-4-8053-1305-3

Distributed by

*North America, Latin America
and Europe*
Tuttle Publishing
364 Innovation Drive
North Clarendon
VT 05759-9436 U.S.A.
Tel: 1 (802) 773-8930
Fax: 1 (802) 773-6993
info@tuttlepublishing.com
www.tuttlepublishing.com

Japan
Tuttle Publishing
Yaekari Building, 3rd Floor
5-4-12 Osaki, Shinagawa-ku
Tokyo 141-0032
Tel: (81) 3 5437-0171
Fax: (81) 3 5437-0755
sales@tuttle.co.jp
www.tuttle.co.jp

Asia Pacific
Berkeley Books Pte. Ltd.
61 Tai Seng Avenue, #02-12
Singapore 534167
Tel: (65) 6280-1330
Fax: (65) 6280-6290
inquiries@periplus.com.sg
www.periplus.com

17 16 15 14
10 9 8 7 6 5 4 3 2

Printed in Singapore
1411 CP

TUTTLE PUBLISHING®
is a registered trademark of
Tuttle Publishing, a division of
Periplus Editions (HK) Ltd.

The Tuttle Story
Books to Span
the East and West

Many people are surprised to learn
that the world's largest publisher
of books on Asia had its humble
beginnings in the tiny American state
of Vermont. The company's founder,
Charles E. Tuttle, belonged to a New
England family steeped in publishing.

Immediately after WWII, Tuttle
served in Tokyo under General
Douglas MacArthur and was
tasked with reviving the Japanese
publishing industry. He later founded
the Charles E. Tuttle Publishing
Company, which thrives today
as one of the world's leading
independent publishers.

Though a westerner, Tuttle was
hugely instrumental in bringing a
knowledge of Japan and Asia to a
world hungry for information about
the East. By the time of his death
in 1993, Tuttle had published over
6,000 books on Asian culture, history
and art—a legacy honored by the
Japanese emperor with the "Order
of the Sacred Treasure," the highest
tribute Japan can bestow upon a
non-Japanese.

With a backlist of 1,500 titles, Tuttle
Publishing is more active today than
at any time in its past—inspired
by Charles Tuttle's core mission to
publish fine books to span the East
and West and provide a greater
understanding of each.